Abou

Martin Cox has taught at prii
surprised when he meets p
to their children! He loves
assemblies. His expertise is
books usually have a strong ᴍ... ....

book, *A Busy Time for Angels*, a big book for the Literacy Hour
published by John Hunt, was a retelling of the Christmas story
from Mary's viewpoint. He also writes songs and carols.

Martin is married with three children. He has been going to
church since he was able to walk there and can't remember a time
when God was not part of his journey. He writes songs because
they keep popping into his head, and plays the piano and different
sizes of recorder. If you want to annoy him, just suggest that the
recorder is an instrument that people only learn until they decide
what proper instrument they want to play. His friends say he talks
a lot and his wife says he even sings in his sleep.

He likes being busy and can't understand people saying they're
bored. When he does sit still, he likes nothing better than to read
both adult and children's books recommended by his friends. It's
the very best way to relax, but you have to learn how not to get
chocolate fingerprints on the pages.

Text copyright © Martin Cox 2007
The author asserts the moral right
to be identified as the author of this work

Published by
The Bible Reading Fellowship
First Floor, Elsfield Hall
15–17 Elsfield Way, Oxford OX2 8FG
Website: www.brf.org.uk

ISBN-10: 1 84101 459 1
ISBN-13: 978 1 84101 459 3
First published 2007
10 9 8 7 6 5 4 3 2 1 0
All rights reserved

Acknowledgments
Unless otherwise stated, scripture quotations are taken from the Contemporary English
Version of the Bible published by HarperCollins Publishers, copyright © 1991, 1992, 1995
American Bible Society.

Scriptures quoted from the Good News Bible published by The Bible Societies/HarperCollins
Publishers Ltd, UK © American Bible Society 1966, 1971, 1976, 1992, used with
permission.

Performance and copyright
The right to perform *Assemblies for Autumn Festivals* drama material is included in the
purchase price, so long as the performance is in an amateur context, for instance in church
services, schools or holiday club venues. Where any charge is made to audiences, written
permission must be obtained from the author, who can be contacted through the publishers.
A fee or royalties may be payable for the right to perform the script in that context.

A catalogue record for this book is available from the British Library

Printed in Singapore by Craft Print International Ltd

Assemblies
for Autumn Festivals

27 ready-to-use ideas for festivals and feast days

Martin Cox

To Will, Sophie and Emily

Contents

Part One: Assemblies for autumn festivals

Part Two: Ideas for cross-curricular work

Part Three: Appendices

Foreword

This book is a very welcome addition to existing resources for autumn term Christian collective worship. It has a clear structure and the themes have been well chosen and resourced. The wide variety of good and easily achievable ideas for engaging and involving pupils is very helpful. Teachers are very well supported by relevant biblical quotations, as well as key background information for each topic and an act of collective worship. All this enriches the book and helps to give a sense of this part of the Christian year.

Martin has devised a valuable resource for collective worship, but this book offers much more. The additional resources linked to various curriculum areas—specifically RE, Citizenship, Literacy, Art and even, in one case, Maths—provide lots more ideas for worship as well as curriculum work in the classroom. This is a rich source of ideas to help teachers develop coherent links between collective worship and lessons.

There is a lot packed into this book and those who read it will find it instantly accessible, its ideas usable and the flexibility it offers extremely valuable. Let's hope Martin will also tackle the spring and summer terms.

Jo Fageant, Oxford Diocese Board of Education
Schools Adviser for South Oxfordshire and Oxford City

Introduction

I hope you enjoy using this book. It's packed with tried and tested ideas for collective worship and the way it has been structured will enable you to use it in a flexible way. You can, of course, dip in and try an occasional assembly that suits your needs, but there are two fuller approaches that will both work well.

Date order

First of all, you might use the assemblies in the order in which they are set out. There are two assemblies in each set (except for Advent, which has five). Either of the assemblies could be presented by a teacher, or one could be expanded—possibly with the use of extra material from Part Two and the appendices—as a class assembly to be presented by the children.

Key themes

Alternatively, you could choose one of the four key themes. Look at the grid on page 11 to see whether this approach appeals to you. The themes, Harvest, Saints, Remembrance and Advent, are expanded in the appendices. Time for thematic work is often limited in school unless clear links are made to Literacy objectives or set units of work—for example, in RE or Citizenship—but many teachers are making more of these links in order to cover the curriculum more efficiently. The extra materials have been gathered so that teachers called upon to put together a class assembly have further material to draw on. Feel free to be creative both with this material and with the original assemblies.

❖

Whatever approach you choose, please take a few moments to read through the background information and decide which of the resources you might choose to use. Sometimes they are essential and at other times purely optional. Some of the assemblies are more interactive, others more visual. Different things may work better in your context and you'll know what to use. So much can now be accessed via the Internet, by using search engines such as google.com or yahoo.com, that we've chosen not to provide illustration templates, but where a particular image came to mind, I may have listed a website as a suggestion. I am very grateful to all at BRF for their endless advice and help while I was preparing the book for publication, especially Sue Doggett, the commissioning editor.

In terms of resources, I've assumed that most schools will have a copy of the BBC book *Come and Praise*. Alongside this, I've often suggested songs from the Out of the Ark *Songs for Every…* series with their super CD backing tracks. There are other useful song-]books that are worth a look, especially *Kidsource* and its adult version, *The Source*. When looking for famous hymns, any traditional hymn book will come in handy. I've referred to *Hymns Old and New* as a source. I've always tried to use a mixture of traditional and modern hymns during a term.

Worksheets

Worksheets 1–8 can be downloaded free of charge from the 'Books and resources' section of the *Barnabas* website:
www.barnabasinschools.org.uk

Ways to use the assemblies

Grid of themes

HARVEST	SAINTS	REMEMBRANCE	ADVENT
Give a man a fish	All Welcome (St Matthew)	Guy Fawkes	The servant king (Christ the King, the Sunday before Advent)
A fair harvest	Forgive us… (St Matthew)	Remember the firework safety code	The kingdom of peace (Isaiah)
Wonderful world (also St Francis)	The story of Michael and the dragon (Michaelmas)	Remembering	The patriarchs
Off to the fair (Michaelmas)	Off to the fair (Michaelmas)	An act of remembrance	The prophets
	Living a simple life (St Francis)		John the Baptist
	Wonderful world (St Francis)		Mary
	Carrying on the work of Jesus (St Luke)		Jesus pitches his tent
	Saying 'thank you' (St Luke)		Three bags of gold (St Nicholas)
	All Saints		
	Gideon, the reluctant hero		
	Passing on the message (St Andrew)		
	Treasure in clay pots (St Andrew)		
	Three bags of gold (St Nicholas)		
	God loves a generous giver (St Nicholas)		

PART ONE

Assemblies for autumn festivals

Harvest

Give a man a fish

The theme of this assembly is helping others to help themselves. Harvest is the final part of a process that starts with the sowing of some of the seed from the previous harvest. Everything that has been grown and safely gathered in (the 'harvest home', as the hymn 'Come you thankful people' puts it) has been cared for by the farmer, and the crops have been watered by God, the Lord of the harvest—a bit like the head gardener in charge of the seasons.

Bible links

I am not trying to make life easier for others by making life harder for you. But it is only fair for you to share with them when you have so much, and they have so little. Later, when they have more than enough, and you are in need, they can share with you. Then everyone will have a fair share.

2 CORINTHIANS 8:13–14

Key background information for the teacher

The apostle Paul, in his second letter to the Christians in Corinth, says that God loves people who give cheerfully (2 Corinthians 9:7b).

Suggestions for visual aids and resources

- A fishing net or a rod and line
- The letters H E L P, each on a separate card
- A poster or OHT with the saying, 'Give a man a fish…'

Ideas for exploring the theme

Start by talking to the children about going fishing and get some of them to share their experiences. Introduce the saying, 'Give a man a fish and feed him for a day. Teach a man to fish and feed him for a lifetime.' Discuss the meaning of this saying.

Ask the children if they know of any charities that help to feed people who are hungry. They might refer to charities that feed the hungry in this country or those that specialize in famine relief. It is important to give value to those charities that attend to people's immediate needs, but also to get the children to see the value of helping people over the longer term. This aid can be given in a variety of ways: helping to educate and train people for work, making people better so that they can earn a living, teaching farming and fishing skills, bringing water to a village, and so on.

You could wordstorm and record ideas with the children around the word CHARITY (another word for love and care) or HELP.

Here is a suggestion for presenting the word HELP, using each of the four letters as a prompt. You could have them ready on four pieces of card for volunteers to hold, revealing them in order.

- **H is for Harvest:** explain what is special about harvest—a time to say thank you to God for all the good things he gives us, and a time when we remind ourselves to share some of what we have with those less fortunate.

- **E is for Everyone:** we are all part of one world, one enormous family, one 'human race'. (One World Week is celebrated by some churches at this time of year.)

● **L is for Love:** a chance to celebrate God's love for us and to show it in our generosity to others. You might focus here on the famous chorus of the harvest hymn 'We plough the fields', which picks up this theme. You could repeat it together to involve the younger children:

All good gifts around us are sent from heaven above.
Then thank the Lord, O thank the Lord, for all his love.

● **P is for Prayer:** when we pray, it is a chance to praise and thank God for all the things we enjoy and to tell him how we feel about the needs of others. We often pray at harvest time for charities that work to make people's lives better, and we can do this now. When we pray, it can change us to make us more generous and kind. (There is a suitable prayer suggested below.)

Suggestions for songs

● When I needed a neighbour (*Come and Praise* 65)
● We plough the fields (*Hymns Old and New* 534)
● Come, you thankful people, come (*Hymns Old and New* 10)
● Pears and apples (*Come and Praise* 135)

Suggested prayer

Dear God, thank you for all the good things we enjoy. Help us, this harvest time, to remember people without enough to eat. Thank you for all the charities that work so hard to help, and for all those people who work for them, both in this country and abroad. Help them to use all the money people give wisely and well, to help as many people as possible, not just when they are hungry but so that they can make a better life for themselves in the future. Amen

Harvest

A fair harvest

This assembly pulls out the theme that as we appreciate the beauty of the world around us and recapture a sense of wonder, we should be drawn back to the amazing God who creates and sustains it. As the 'crown' of God's created order, we have been entrusted with the responsibility to care for the world, and alongside that responsibility run God's frequent commands to treat others with justice and fairness.

Bible links

You take care of the earth and send rain to help the soil grow all kinds of crops.

PSALM 65:9a

I often think of the heavens your hands have made, and of the moon and stars you put in place... You let us rule everything your hands have made. And you put all of it under our power—the sheep and the cattle, and every wild animal, the birds in the sky, the fish in the sea, and all ocean creatures.

PSALM 8:3 and 6–8

Key background information for the teacher

The Bible presents us with a God who has created a beautiful world, which he has entrusted to human beings for its safekeeping. Harvest is a time when we thank God with a sense of awe and wonder, while recognizing that we don't always share the resources fairly. We also clearly have an unnerving ability to mess the world up. The Bible regards those who believe in God as stewards with a responsibility to look after the created world and to work towards a fairer distribution of its resources.

These themes are developed further in the appendix on page 162, which contains many ideas for classroom links.

Suggestions for visual aids and resources

- ○ Some fruit (such as an apple, raisins, or a banana)
- ○ The letters H A R V E S T, each on a separate card

Ideas for exploring the theme

Start by asking the children, 'How many of you like the fruit you see here?' (You could show them examples of different fruits and ask which are grown in this country and which abroad.) Say that nowadays we can send food all over the world very quickly and enjoy fruit from lots of countries, even when it is 'out of season' in our own country.

Explain that in today's assembly you will be thinking about how many people in the world do not have enough to eat, while we are able to eat things that have been brought here as a matter of course. We needn't feel guilty about this, because growing, packing and transporting our food gives work to lots of people (although many people have growing concerns about fuel usage and carbon emissions). It is worth thinking about whether we can make the process more fair—making sure that fewer people struggle to get the basic food they need, and that those who grow our food all over the world get paid a fair price for the food they grow.

You could get some volunteers to hold up the letters of the word HARVEST, but not in the right order. Depending on the age of the children, you can make this easier or harder, scrambling the letters up completely or putting some of the volunteers in the correct positions.

Once the children have guessed the word HARVEST, ask if they can use some of the letters to create other shorter words. Among others, you should get the following words:

HAVE
SHARE
VAST
REST

Out of these, you should be able to improvise some thoughts about how the **vast** world we live in produces enough food so that no one need go hungry, but those who **have** the most need to be more thoughtful about how to **share** the world's resources with the **rest**, who are often hungry—even those who grow food themselves.

(Be prepared for the words 'vest' and 'star' to be suggested, both of which you could perhaps use with a little ingenuity. I haven't yet come up with a way to weave in the word 'shave'!)

Possible ways to comment further will depend on your local circumstances. For example, you could mention at this point that harvest is often the time when we are most aware of those in need, both in this country and abroad. Maybe the food collected at your school's harvest festival is boxed up for a local charity that works with the homeless, or is sent to local elderly people to put a smile on their faces—reminding the children that their school is at the centre of their community. It may be that you are collecting for a charity such as Christian Aid or Send a Cow (see page 176 for contact details). This could be an opportunity to highlight how anything with a Fairtrade mark on it helps those who grow the food in poorer countries by ensuring that more of the profit goes back to the grower. If everyone bought just one item of Fairtrade produce when doing the weekly shop, it would make a huge difference to people's lives.

Suggestions for songs

- ❁ All things bright and beautiful (*Come and Praise* 3)
- ❁ When I needed a neighbour (*Come and Praise* 65)

See the full list of suggestions for songs on page 167 of the appendix.

Suggested prayer

Father God, we thank you for our daily food. We remember those who do not have enough to eat. We ask you to make us more grateful for what we have and less selfish. Give your wisdom and strength to those who are helping to change the world into a fairer place to live. Amen

✣

Matthew: apostle and evangelist

Assembly 1

All welcome

This assembly aims to reinforce the idea that each of us is special to God. He loves each individual uniquely, and particularly wants to reach out to those who don't feel close to God or who feel in need of his friendship. God doesn't put up barriers as we sometimes do when we discover that people are 'not our type' or are different in some way that we consider significant.

Bible links

Jesus... saw a tax collector named Matthew sitting at the place for paying taxes. Jesus said to him, 'Come with me.' Matthew got up and went with him. Later, Jesus and his disciples were having dinner at Matthew's house. Many tax collectors and other sinners were also there. Some Pharisees asked Jesus' disciples, 'Why does your teacher eat with tax collectors and other sinners?' Jesus heard them and answered, 'Healthy people don't need a doctor, but sick people do. Go and learn what the Scriptures mean when they say, "Instead of offering sacrifices to me, I want you to be merciful to others." I didn't come to invite good people to be my followers. I came to invite sinners.'
MATTHEW 9:9–13

The kingdom of heaven is like what happened when a king gave a wedding banquet for his son. The king sent some servants to tell the invited guests to come to the banquet, but the guests refused. He sent other servants to say to the guests, 'The banquet is ready! My cattle and prize calves have all been prepared. Everything is ready. Come to the banquet!'

But the guests did not pay any attention. Some of them left for their farms, and some went to their places of business...

Then he said to the servants, 'It is time for the wedding banquet, and the invited guests don't deserve to come. Go out to the street corners and tell everyone you meet to come to the banquet.' They went out into the streets and brought in everyone they could find, good and bad alike. And the banquet room was filled with guests.

MATTHEW 22:2–5 and 8–10

Key background information for the teacher

Jesus stated clearly that he had a particular role to play, inviting back to God those who felt on the edge of society or who, for a variety of reasons, had gone off track. He compared it to needing a doctor. Those who know they are unwell are ready to visit the doctor and to follow his advice. Matthew was a tax collector, in the pay of the occupying Roman army—a double reason for people to dislike him.

Suggestions for visual aids and resources

- ✪ A sign or banner saying ALL WELCOME. (You might have a doormat with something similar on it!)
- ✪ Three children who are different from each other, for example, in height, hairstyle, eye colour and so on. (Make sure they don't mind being featured.)
- ✪ The Bible passages printed above

Ideas for exploring the theme

Ask for three volunteers (if you haven't organized this in advance). Ask the other children to point out differences between them. Ask the children whether, if Jesus came to meet them, he would treat any one of them differently from the others. Clearly not! Ask how they think Jesus would react if one of the volunteers had done something wrong. Tease out the idea that, just like when adults in school have to sort out children's poor behaviour, it's the behaviour that Jesus would dislike, not the person.

Ask the children to listen to a Bible reading about Jesus inviting Matthew to leave his job and become one of his helpers. It might help to know that everybody has to pay taxes, but at the time when Jesus was born the Romans had taken over the Jewish land and Matthew was working for the Romans. He was the sort of person that other people didn't like much.

Read the Bible passage from Matthew 9 (see above). Who was Jesus interested in meeting and helping? *(Those who knew they needed God's help and a new start in life; those who knew they needed to hear that God loved them.)* It was a bit like going to the doctor's: some people go just for a medical check-up, but know they feel fine; others go knowing that they need some help and advice. When people turned up to see Jesus, they might have found a welcome mat or a sign saying ALL WELCOME.

If there is time, you could also draw the children's attention to the parable Jesus told about a king who invited guests to his son's wedding (see above). When the time came for the guests to arrive, they all were busy elsewhere and didn't turn up, so the king sent his servants out to invite those who wouldn't have expected an invitation. (Some people see this as a picture of God making sure that the Jewish people, whom he has worked with throughout history, have a chance to respond first to the new invitation that Jesus brings, but then all others are also welcome to come to the party.)

This parable works well as one of those stories in which the children respond to certain key words by adding actions. Here are some possibilities:

- ✪ King = put crown on head
- ✪ Servant = pretend to hold a tray of drinks on the flat of your hand like a waiter
- ✪ Guest = smarten yourself up (tighten your tie or tidy your hair)
- ✪ Banquet = pretend to pull a party popper (with or without sound effects)

This is a very effective way of telling the story while involving the children. If you are feeling brave, you can add actions that have sound! When reading the parable, use a version of the Bible that is accessible to the children (such as the CEV above) and practise beforehand.

You might want to repeat briefly the idea that each of us is special and invited to get to know God better. You could explain that this will be the content of the prayer at the end of the assembly.

Suggestions for songs

- ✪ God knows me (*Come and Praise* 15)
- ✪ He'll be there (a version of Psalm 139) (*Songs for Every Assembly*, Out of the Ark)

Suggested prayer

Thank you, God, for the reminder today that each one of us is important to you and that you want each one of us to get to know you better. Help us not to shy away from others who are different from us, but to treat others as special too. Amen

Matthew: apostle and evangelist

<(Assembly 2)>

Forgive us...

This assembly really brings home the line in the Lord's Prayer about forgiveness. When we are forgiven ourselves, we should show the same level of forgiveness, or greater, to others.

Bible links

Peter came up to the Lord and asked, 'How many times should I forgive someone who does something wrong to me? Is seven times enough?' Jesus answered: Not just seven times, but seventy times seven! This story will show you what the kingdom of heaven is like:

One day a king decided to call in his officials and ask them to give an account of what they owed him. As he was doing this, one official was brought in who owed him fifty million silver coins. But he didn't have any money to pay what he owed. The king ordered him to be sold, along with his wife and children and all he owned, in order to pay the debt.

The official got down on his knees and began begging, 'Have pity on me, and I will pay you every penny I owe!' The king felt sorry for him and let him go free. He even told the official that he did not have to pay back the money.

As the official was leaving, he happened to meet another official, who owed him a hundred silver coins. So he grabbed the man by the throat. He started choking him and said, 'Pay me what you owe!'

The man got down on his knees and began begging, 'Have pity on me, and I will pay you back.' But the first official refused to have pity. Instead, he went and had the other official put in jail until he could pay what he owed.

When some other officials found out what had happened, they felt sorry for the man who had been put in jail. Then they told the king what had happened. The king called the first official back in and said, 'You're an evil man! When you begged for mercy, I said you did not have to pay back a penny. Don't you think you should show pity to someone else, as I did to you?' The king was so angry that he ordered the official to be tortured until he could pay back everything he owed. That is how my Father in heaven will treat you, if you don't forgive each of my followers with all your heart.

MATTHEW 18:21–35

Key background information for the teacher

Jesus often taught through parables, using simple imagery to make his point. Parables are scattered throughout the Gospels, but some are unique to Matthew, such as the story about the farmer and the valuable pearl (both in Matthew 13, which is packed with 'kingdom' parables) and the story of the workers in a vineyard in Matthew 20 (which features in one of our Michaelmas assemblies).

This assembly highlights another parable that appears only in Matthew's Gospel: the story of the official who refused to forgive. In replying that Peter should forgive 490 times, I think that Jesus was suggesting an unlimited number of times. Surely, by then, the ability to forgive would become an essential part of a person's make-up.

Suggestions for visual aids and resources

✪ A calculator or, even better, an OHP calculator

Ideas for exploring the theme

Begin by asking the children some multiplication questions, getting increasingly difficult, to involve the youngest through to the oldest children. Include the questions 1 x 7 and 70 x 7. Also include some that require further understanding of place value, such as 3 x 10, 3 x 100, 3 x 10,000 and so on, including 3 x 1,000,000. You could make it a competition or get someone to check each answer with a calculator. An OHP calculator would make the progression from 30 to 3,000,000 more obvious still.

Now ask the question, 'If someone did something to annoy or hurt you, would you be able to forgive them?' *(Perhaps.)* 'What if they did the same thing again?' *(Harder to do.)*

Explain how Matthew's Gospel records that Peter came to Jesus with a difficult question about how many times we should forgive someone. He asked if he should go up to 7 times, but Jesus suggested 70 x 7. As so often, Jesus followed up his answer with a story, and this one is about an official who refused to forgive. It's a lively one to act out. You might choose to prepare a group beforehand so that the story is familiar to them and they don't overdo the strangling!

Read from a Bible version that is easy to understand (such as the CEV above). Alternatively, prepare children with the script on page 28. Jesus was keen to point out that God wants us to treat others as we want to be treated. He felt so strongly about it that he said lack of forgiveness would be punished. The first servant was guilty of what we call hypocrisy and of falling short of God's standards. Let's hope that we will be quick to forgive other people, as this will please God.

Suggestions for songs

❂ Our Father, who art in heaven (*Come and Praise* 51)

Suggested prayer

Say the Lord's Prayer (introduce it by asking children to listen out for the line about forgiveness).

Narrator:	Once there was a king who decided to check up on the money he had lent to his servants. Just as he began to do this, one of them was brought in who owed him 50 million silver coins. The servant obviously didn't have enough money to pay what he owed, so the king decided he should be sold as a slave, along with his family and all his possessions, in order to pay off the debt.
Servant 1:	Be patient with me, Your Majesty, and I'll pay you everything I owe.
Narrator:	The king felt sorry for the servant as he knelt before him, begging.
King:	I release you from the debt. Now go.
Narrator:	As he went out, the man met one of his fellow servants who owed him just one hundred silver coins. He grabbed him by the throat.
Servant 1:	You! Pay me what you owe me.
Servant 2:	Be patient with me and I'll pay you everything I owe.
Servant 1:	No way! You can be locked up until you pay up!
Narrator:	The other servants reported back to the king what they had seen and heard, so he called the first servant back.
King:	You're nothing but a worthless slave. I forgave you the whole debt you owed me—millions of silver coins—when you asked me for mercy, but you showed no forgiveness to your fellow servant who owed you so much less. You're the one who should be locked up. Take him off to jail!

Reproduced with permission from *Assemblies for Autumn Festivals* published by BRF 2007 (1 84101 459 1)
www.barnabasinschools.org.uk

✤

Michaelmas (the feast of St Michael and All Angels)

The story of Michael and the dragon

The angel Michael has a special day dedicated to him at this time of year. The story of Michael brings out an important aspect of the work of angels—protection. For this reason, angels are often regarded as guardians. This theme explores the need to be brave, the conviction that good is stronger than evil and the concept of God having absolute power and ultimately winning the battle between good and evil. This is a major theme in the Bible.

Bible links

A war broke out in heaven. Michael and his angels were fighting against the dragon and its angels. But the dragon lost the battle. It and its angels were forced out of their places in heaven and were thrown down to the earth. Yes, that old snake and his angels were thrown out of heaven! That snake, who fools everyone on earth, is known as the devil and Satan. Then I heard a voice from heaven shout, 'Our God has shown his saving power, and his kingdom has come! God's own Chosen One has shown his authority. Satan accused our people in the presence of God day and night. Now he has been thrown out! Our people defeated Satan because of the blood [or death] of the Lamb and the message of God. They were willing to give up their lives. The heavens should rejoice, together with everyone who lives there. But pity the earth and the sea, because the devil was thrown down to the earth. He knows his time is short, and he is very angry.'

REVELATION 12:7–12

Key background information for the teacher

This passage paints a picture of the battle between good and evil. The account portrays quite a frightening scene, in which Michael acts as the leader of the angels of good against the angels of darkness, who are thrown out of heaven with their leader, Satan.

Suggestions for visual aids and resources

○ An example of a job description from a newspaper
○ Pictures of angels, including, if possible, the one of Michael and the devil from Coventry Cathedral (see www.coventrycathedral.org.uk)
○ A sign saying GOOD v. evil; LOVE v. hate

Ideas for exploring the theme

Begin by asking the children what qualifications you need for a particular job. For example, what qualifications would you need to be a doctor or a teacher? Show or read out one or two job descriptions from the newspaper.

Explain that the assembly today is about angels. Ask if the children know what angels are. What might we put in their job description? Key ideas to tease out might include an ability to remember and deliver messages, an ability to follow orders and the need to be punctual. Children might also mention a polished halo, a good sense of direction and an ability to fly. All the suggestions given will help to build a picture of the children's perception of what angels are.

Explain that angels are often mentioned in the Bible. Do the children know the names of any biblical angels? The most well known is the angel Gabriel, who brought an important message to Mary, that she would be the mother of Jesus.

Tell the children that another angel mentioned in the Bible is the angel Michael, who fought a battle in heaven between good and evil. If possible, show them the image of the archangel Michael's struggle with Satan, which is on the wall by the main entrance to Coventry Cathedral. You could describe it. St Michael has struggled with God's enemy, the devil, and now stands on him. It is a sign of the struggle between good and evil. God's angel Michael has won the fight. This image can be found on the Coventry Cathedral website: www.coventrycathedral.org.uk.

Introduce the theme of good and evil by holding up a sign that reads: GOOD v. evil; LOVE v. hate. Explain that Christians believe that God is everything that is good. and that God is everything that is love. The Bible teaches that good is stronger than evil and that love is stronger than hate.

Encourage the children to look at the words and notice that some of them are in capitals to remind us of this important truth. They could continue to look at the sign while you tell the story of Michael fighting the dragon, from Revelation 12:7–12 (see above).

Suggestions for songs

○ One more step (*Junior Praise* 188; *Come and Praise* 47)
○ When a knight won his spurs (*Kidsource* 371)
○ My God is so big (*Junior Praise* 169)

Suggested prayer

Encourage the children to add the 'Amen' if they agree with the prayer.

Father God, thank you for the story of the angel Michael, which reminds us that GOOD is stronger than evil and that LOVE is stronger than hate. Help us to remember that the kingdom, the power and the glory are yours, now and for ever. Amen

Alternatively, or as an addition to the above prayer, you might wish to use the Lord's Prayer in its traditional or modern form. Explain to the children that the final lines pick up the theme of this assembly.

‧∴‧

Michaelmas (the feast of St Michael and All Angels)

Assembly 2

Off to the fair

September and October are popular times for travelling fairs. They are often called Michaelmas fairs, or goose fairs. Goose fairs often take place between 29 September (Michaelmas) and 11 October.

Bible links

The Kingdom of heaven is like this. Once there was a man who went out early in the morning to hire some men to work in his vineyard. He agreed to pay them the regular wage, a silver coin a day, and sent them to work in his vineyard. He went out again to the market place at nine o'clock and saw some men standing there doing nothing, so he told them, 'You also go and work in the vineyard, and I will pay you a fair wage.' So they went. Then at twelve o'clock and again at three o'clock he did the same thing. It was nearly five o'clock when he went to the market place and saw some other men still standing there. 'Why are you wasting the whole day here doing nothing?' he asked them. 'No one hired us,' they answered. 'Well, then, you also go and work in the vineyard,' he told them.

When evening came, the owner told his foreman, 'Call the workers and pay them their wages, starting with those who were hired last and ending with those who were hired first.' The men who had begun to work at five o'clock were paid a silver coin each. So when the men who were the first to be hired came to be paid, they thought they would get more; but they too were given a silver coin each. They took their money and started grumbling against the employer. 'These men who were hired last worked only one hour,' they said, 'while we put up with a whole day's work in the hot sun—yet you paid them the same as you paid us!'

'Listen, friend,' the owner answered one of them, 'I have not cheated you. After all, you agreed to do a day's work for one silver coin. Now take your pay and go home. I want to give this man who was hired last as much as I have given you. Don't I have the right to do as I wish with my own money? Or are you jealous because I am generous?'

MATTHEW 20:1–15 (GNB)

Key background information for the teacher

Hundreds of years ago, a medieval fair was a mixture of entertainment, buying, selling and business. These fairs were sometimes called goose fairs, due to the animals brought there for sale, or hiring fairs because people paid their rents there and it was a good time to choose new workers.

Suggestions for visual aids and resources

- ❁ A CD of the song 'Scarborough Fair' sung by Simon and Garfunkel, to play as the children enter
- ❁ A bunch of grapes
- ❁ A wine bottle
- ❁ An advert for a fair (optional)

Ideas for exploring the theme

Ask the children what they would expect to find at a fair. Talk about what fairs were like in medieval times. Ask the children if they know what grows in a vineyard. You could use the grapes and the wine bottle as visual aids to explain how wine is made. It may also be a good idea to check that the children understand the ideas of rent and hiring before you get too far into the assembly.

Introduce the story of the workers in the vineyard and tell the story briefly in your own words or using a modern translation of the Bible (such as the GNB above, or the CEV). You could make the story interactive by inviting the children to add actions. Before telling the story, practise some actions for the children to do every time you mention certain key words in the text. This will keep them involved and help them to remember the story. For example:

Pay = put hand to pocket, then offer pretend money.

Vineyard = drink from a glass (you could add 'cheers!').

Work = wipe the sweat from your brow.

Look at your watch whenever the time is mentioned in the story. You could comment on the story by explaining that God treats everyone generously, whether they have worked for him a long time or only been friends with him a short time. Christians believe that it is part of God's nature to be not simply fair, but also kind and generous. The story isn't really about money; it's about love and generosity.

Suggestions for songs

◎ Jesus' love is very wonderful (*Kidsource* 208)
◎ God is love, his the care (*Come and Praise* 36)

Suggested prayer

Father God, thank you that you are generous and want everyone to be friends with you. Help us to be friendly, forgiving and caring to others too. Amen

✣

St Francis of Assisi

⟨ **Assembly 1** ⟩

Living a simple life

The feast of St Francis is celebrated on 4 October. As well as standing alone, this assembly, alongside its partner 'Wonderful world', would link to a series on saints or to one on Harvest, depending on the emphasis. This assembly shows that Francis was someone who listened and acted when he was challenged by the words of the Bible.

Bible links

As you go, announce that the kingdom of heaven will soon be here. Heal the sick, raise the dead to life, heal people who have leprosy, and force out demons. You received without paying, now give without being paid. Don't take along any gold, silver, or copper coins. And don't carry a travelling bag or an extra shirt or sandals or a walking stick. Workers deserve their food.

MATTHEW 10:7–10

Key background information for the teacher

Francis was born into a wealthy family but gave up his life of privilege to devote himself to prayer and to helping people who were living in poverty. Research shows that, time and again, authors have referred to him as the most popular saint of the Middle Ages. He is often named as the saint who behaved most like Jesus.

The definition of a saint is someone who led a particularly holy life and who, as a Christian, dedicated their life to serving others. Francis certainly lives up to this definition. The New Testament refers to each Christian as a saint and, for us, people such as St Francis set an example to follow as we travel through life as 'saints in the making'.

Some of the characteristics of St Francis that deserve noting are that he lived simply, cared for those who were unwell, told others the message about Jesus and loved the natural world created by God. In addition, he developed the stigmata later in life. This means that the marks of the crucifixion appeared on his body (although he tried not to draw attention to them).

Francis is also famous for inventing the idea of the Christmas crib. He wanted to get across to the local people the sort of conditions into which Jesus was born, so he organized what might be called a 'live manger scene' with real animals. You could elaborate on this event in his life if you present the assembly about Francis after All Saints, in the period when you are preparing for Christmas celebrations. You could perhaps discuss why we act out a nativity play or use a Christmas crib scene to remind us of the events of the first Christmas. These events lie at the true centre of our celebrations, however much other Christmas customs have added to the season.

Francis' most famous piece of writing is 'The canticle of the sun', which could usefully be performed at a Harvest service or assembly. It works well as choral speech and could be prepared in a Literacy lesson. A version can be found on pages 43–44.

Suggestions for visual aids and resources

- Dressing-up clothes. You could have two children ready to be Francis in smart clothes and the beggar in ragged clothes. They could act out the story (see below) or you could simply tell it.
- Prepare a card for someone to read, with the words of Matthew 10:7–10 that changed Francis' life (see 'Bible links' on page 36).

Ideas for exploring the theme

Explain to the children that there are many special days in the church calendar when we are encouraged to remember saints—special people who followed the teaching of Jesus and led lives that set us a good example. One of these saints is Francis, whose special day is 4 October.

Explain the key idea of the assembly—that Francis was so moved when he heard part of the Bible being read that he knew he had to change the way he was living.

Relate an event in Francis' life when he went on a pilgrimage to Rome, where the leader of the Church, the Pope, lived. He was very upset by the sight of so many beggars at the Pope's church, St Peter's. (*This is where you could add actors.*) Francis did something quite unusual: he asked to swap clothes for a day with one of the beggars, so that he could feel what it was like to be penniless and have to beg for food. It was very different from the sort of life he had known while growing up. When he went back home, he decided to spend his time looking after people with a skin disease called leprosy.

When Francis was at church one day, he heard a reading from Matthew's Gospel, chapter 10, verses 7–10. (*Read the passage. Someone could read it for you as if reading the Bible in church.*) Francis decided, from that point on, to live a more simple life. He took off his shoes and went around barefoot. He put on a long hooded cloak, tied round the waist with a simple rope belt. He then went around, telling everyone the message about Jesus.

Suggestions for songs

○ When I needed a neighbour (*Come and Praise* 65)
○ Would you walk by on the other side? (*Come and Praise* 70)
○ Spirit of God (*Come and Praise* 63)
○ Make me a channel of your peace (*Come and Praise* 147)

Suggested prayer

Father God, help us to listen well when we hear your words from the Bible read to us. Help us to know when you want us to change something in the way we live and behave, so that we might love people in the way Jesus did. Amen

This is a prayer often associated with St Francis:

Lord, make me an instrument of your peace,
Where there is hatred, let me sow love;
where there is injury, pardon;
where there is doubt, faith;
where there is despair, hope;
where there is darkness, light;
where there is sadness, joy;

O Divine Master, grant that I may not so much seek
to be consoled as to console;
to be understood as to understand;
to be loved as to love.

For it is in giving that we receive;
it is in pardoning that we are pardoned;
and it is in dying that we are born to eternal life.

You could use part of this prayer or use the version found in many song books.

Below is a simplified version of the Collect (special prayer for the day) used in church about St Francis.

O God, you love to show people what you are like, and you especially like to welcome children to come to you, to get to know you better. May we be more like St Francis, who was not so interested in gaining knowledge for its own sake but wanted to understand more about Jesus and how you wanted us all to live. We praise you, Father, Son and Holy Spirit. Amen

St Francis of Assisi

Wonderful world

For many people, it is a natural response to the beauty of the world to want to praise God, or at least to ask questions about how it all came about. Even many people without a faith in God admit to a sense of awe, being moved to question whether the world they see points back to a creative force. Christians recognize this response in their harvest celebrations, when they focus not just on praising God for the beauty of the world, but also on our responsibility to be stewards of the world. It is also a point at which Christians are keen to acknowledge the creativity of God, which has been passed on to us. So many fine songs, paintings and pieces of music have been created to capture the awesomeness of the world we live in.

Bible links

Our Lord and Ruler, your name is wonderful everywhere on earth! You let your glory be seen in the heavens above.
PSALM 8:1

Shout praises to the Lord! Shout the Lord's praises in the highest heavens. All you angels, and all who serve him above, come and offer praise. Sun and moon, and all you bright stars, come and offer praise. Highest heavens, and the water above the highest heavens, come and offer praise. Let all things praise the name of the Lord, because they were created at his command.

PSALM 148:1–5

Key background information for the teacher

St Francis is well known for his appreciation of the natural world and our place as one of God's creations within it. In KS2 Science, the children learn about food chains, each of which is a list of consumers with the producer at the start (usually a plant of some kind that has relied on the sun, the earth and water to grow).

This assembly could be used as the basis for a Harvest celebration. Please refer to pages 128–138 for ideas for class work on the theme, many of which could be used to create your own individual assembly and harvest festival.

Suggestions for visual aids and resources

⊙ Elton John's 'Circle of life' (from *The Lion King*) or 'What a wonderful world' (most famously sung by Louis Armstrong, although there are other versions, such as one by Alison Moyet)
⊙ The parts of a food chain on separate cards, including the sun. You could have an arrow sign to connect each part of the chain to the next (to denote 'is food for…')

Ideas for exploring the theme

If you have it, play the song from *The Lion King* (if you have it on video or DVD, you could play it through the TV) or a recording of 'What a wonderful world'. Explain that today in assembly we are going to think about the way many things in the world are linked to each other, and that we humans have a special job to do. Often, it is only in Art that we look closely at how amazing the world is, with its tiny details—such as the patterns on tree bark or flowers. Or perhaps it is in Science, as we discover more about the world, that we begin to think about how humans and different plants and animals are connected.

Use the food chain cards to construct a food chain with help from the children. Explain that even the producer at the beginning is reliant on the sun for light and energy.

One person who recognized how we all rely on the created world was St Francis. Not only did he try to get people to appreciate the beauty of the world that he believed God had created, but he also showed how, as humans (and the most important part of God's creation), we are responsible for looking after everything. He had a particular care for animals and their welfare.

Francis wrote a special poem of celebration, which is often called 'The canticle of the sun'. The poem could be performed at this point by a group of children who have prepared it, or you could read it yourself. The version below is my own paraphrase.

The canticle of the sun

Praise to my Lord God for all his creatures, especially for our brother the sun, who brings us the day and who brings us the light—he is fair and shines with great splendour.

Praise to my Lord God for our sister the moon and for the stars which he set out so clearly in the heavens.

Praise to my Lord for our brother the wind, for the air and clouds and all weather by which life is sustained for all creatures.

Praise to my Lord God for our sister water, so precious and clean, who is so important to us.

Praise to my Lord God for our brother fire, so mighty, bright and strong, through whom you give us light in the darkness.

Praise to my Lord for our mother the earth, from whom come all kinds of fruit and flowers of so many colours for our needs and pleasure.

Praise and bless the Lord, give him your thanks and serve him with humility.

Children could be allowed a few moments to reflect on this poem and to picture the greatness and beauty of the world ·before you conclude the assembly. A prayer and song can also be introduced.

Suggestions for songs

❂ All the nations of the earth (*Come and Praise* 14)
❂ All things bright and beautiful (*Come and Praise* 3)

Suggested prayer

This is part of a prayer by Saint Francis.

Bless the Lord, all you works of the Lord. Let us praise and glorify him for ever. Let heaven and earth praise your glory, all creatures on earth and under the earth, the sea and everything in it. Let us praise and glorify him for ever. Amen

A Jewish prayer:

If my lips could sing as many songs as there are waves in the sea,
If my tongue could sing as many hymns as there are ocean billows,
If my mouth filled the whole firmament (world) with praise,
If my face shone like the sun and moon together,
If my hands were to hover in the sky like powerful eagles
and my feet ran across mountains as swiftly as the deer,
all that would not be enough to pay you fitting tribute,
O Lord my God.

ANON. FROM *THE LION PRAYER COLLECTION*, LION HUDSON

You could adapt the chorus of 'All things bright and beautiful' as follow, to use as a prayer:

All things bright and beautiful, all creatues great and small, all things wise and wonderful—we thank you for them all. Amen

Look for other prayers celebrating God's greatness, such as those in *The Lion Prayer Collection* There are some super ones in the sections entitled 'Telling God's greatness' and 'The world around us'.

✥

Luke the evangelist

Carrying on the work of Jesus

Before Jesus finished his time on earth, he promised that he would send his disciples his Holy Spirit, to help them to remember all that he had taught them and to enable them to continue doing his work. The healing of the lame man (Acts 3) is used by Peter as an opportunity to tell people about Jesus. This story is recorded by Luke, who wrote the book of the Acts of the Apostles. The apostles were the pioneers who established the early church.

Bible links

Many people have tried to tell the story of what God has done among us. They wrote what we had been told by the ones who were there in the beginning and saw what happened. So I made a careful study of everything and then decided to write and tell you exactly what took place. Honourable Theophilus, I have done this to let you know the truth about what you have heard.
LUKE 1:1–4

Ask and you will receive, search and you will find, knock and the door will be opened for you… As bad as you are, you still know how to give good gifts to your children. But your heavenly Father is even more ready to give the Holy Spirit to anyone who asks.
LUKE 11:9 and 13

Theophilus, I first wrote to you about all that Jesus did and taught from the very first until he was taken up to heaven. But before he was taken up, he gave orders to the apostles he had chosen with the help of the Holy Spirit. For forty days after Jesus had suffered and died, he proved in many ways that he had been raised from death. He appeared to his apostles and spoke to them about God's kingdom. While he was still with them, he said: Don't leave Jerusalem yet. Wait here for the Father to give you the Holy Spirit, just as I told you he has promised to do. John baptized with water, but in a few days you will be baptized with the Holy Spirit.

ACTS 1:1–5

Peter and John were on their way to the temple to pray one afternoon, entering through the door known as the Beautiful Gate. There was a beggar who always used this spot. As he was lame, his friends brought him there each morning. When he saw Peter and John, he asked for money to buy food. Peter's reply surprised him: 'I haven't any money but I can give you something I do have. In the name of Jesus Christ of Nazareth, I order you to get up and walk.' Peter reached out his hand to help the man up.

I suppose the man had a choice at that moment, whether to believe Peter or not, but he did reach out in trust and take Peter's hand. At once his feet and ankles became strong and he started to walk around. At last he could get into the temple by himself. He ran about, praising God. People who recognized him were amazed. This gave Peter a chance to tell them what had happened and where the power to heal had come from. 'Do you remember Jesus?' he asked them, and reminded everyone how Jesus had died and been raised to life. 'This man is well because we believe in Jesus and asked God to heal him. The promises God made to you through his prophets are for you to believe as God's people. Turn away from your sins and believe in Jesus.'

ACTS 3:1–10 (AUTHOR'S PARAPHRASE)

Key background information for the teacher

The book we call Acts is a continuation of the Gospel of Luke. It records the establishment of the early churches as the good news ('gospel') about Jesus spread in Jerusalem, across the country, and then around the Mediterranean world including, of course, Rome. A key feature of the book is the work of some of Jesus' closest followers and Saul (later renamed Paul) in this missionary task, equipped and guided by the Holy Spirit. The Christian faith is explained as the fulfilment of the Jewish religion. The new believers are encouraged to continue the work of Jesus in telling people of God's love and expecting God to heal people 'in the name of Jesus'.

Luke has a real eye for a human interest story and makes clear his intention to write an orderly account that explains the truth about Jesus. There is some unique material in his Gospel about the life of Jesus, but we are especially grateful to him for his record in Acts of the lives of those first Christians and their emerging leadership.

Suggestions for visual aids and resources

❂ A pair of trainers
❂ 10p, 50p and some £1 coins

Ideas for exploring the theme

Ask for a couple of volunteers. Ask the first how they would feel if they asked for new trainers, but were given just one of the pair and told to wait for the other until next month. Ask the second volunteer how they would feel if they asked for money to buy an ice cream but were given just 10p. Then ask the first volunteer how they would feel if they asked for a spare pair of trainers, and were given the latest style. Ask the second how they would feel if they asked for 50p, but were given £2.00 and told to keep the change. Thank the volunteers and explain that the story today is about somebody who asked some of Jesus' followers for money and was rather surprised at how much more he received.

Explain to the children that before Jesus went back into heaven, he promised to send his Holy Spirit. The Holy Spirit would help his friends to remember everything he had taught them and give them the power to carry on the work he had been doing among them. Jesus had already trained his closest friends to pray and to heal people. Now the first Christians found that this was happening to them as Jesus promised. When they believed the words of Jesus and prayed for people, healings took place, and these gave Jesus' followers a chance to tell people all about their God.

Introduce the story from Acts 3:1–10 by using a suitable Bible version or the paraphrase above. Wow! The man certainly got more than he expected. He asked for money to buy food and instead got healed—all because Jesus' followers took Jesus' words seriously and believed that God wanted them to carry on the work he had been doing.

Suggestions for songs

❂ Make me a channel of your peace (*Come and Praise* 147)
❂ Peter and John went to pray (*Kidsource* 281)

Suggested prayer

Father God, thank you for Jesus, who helped so many people. Thank you that you promised to give your friends your Holy Spirit to carry on your work. Please help us to believe that you can still use people today to do exciting things for you. Amen

✤

Luke the evangelist

Saying 'thank you'

This is an opportunity to explore the theme of being grateful, and to see how our gratitude should lead to action in saying 'thank you' to those who help us and care for us. Jesus is a supreme example of someone who cared for people in need, especially those who felt unwanted or marginalized. Some explanation is required about what leprosy is and about the customs of the day, but this should not be the main focus. Time should be allowed for children to reflect on the people they are grateful for.

Bible links

On his way to Jerusalem, Jesus went along the border between Samaria and Galilee. As he was going into a village, ten men with leprosy came towards him. They stood at a distance and shouted, 'Jesus, Master, have pity on us!' Jesus looked at them and said, 'Go and show yourselves to the priests.' On their way they were healed. When one of them discovered that he was healed, he came back, shouting praises to God. He bowed down at the feet of Jesus and thanked him. The man was from the country of Samaria. Jesus asked, 'Weren't ten men healed? Where are the other nine? Why was this foreigner the only one who came back to thank God?' Then Jesus told the man, 'You may get up and go. Your faith has made you well.'

LUKE 17:11–19

Key background information for the teacher

Samaria was a region between Judea and Galilee. There were big differences between the Jews and Samaritans in terms of customs, worship, race and politics. There was much bad feeling and suspicion between the two groups. This story is another example of Jesus mixing with people who were on the edge of society not just because they were lepers, but also because they were Samaritans.

There are several stories that are told only in Luke's Gospel— human interest stories that deal with this very issue—showing Jesus making contact with those on the margins and reminding us that God's love reaches far and wide, beyond our typical boundaries. Examples are the parable of the good Samaritan (Luke 10:25–37), the parable of the two sons (Luke 15:11–32) and the account of Jesus at the home of Simon the Pharisee (Luke 7:36–50). Many people think that Luke was a doctor, so he would naturally have been interested in disease and in healing as well as focusing on how Jesus dealt with people.

Suggestions for visual aids and resources

⊕ A card with the words 'Thank you' on it
⊕ You could also use a thought bubble on a garden cane (a large oval piece of card, with some smaller ones underneath) for the 'hot-seating' activity, when children volunteer their thoughts about the characters. There is a thought bubble template on page 173.

Ideas for exploring the theme

Tell the story of the ten lepers. Explain that a leper had a skin disease called leprosy. It was possible to catch this disease if you spent a long time with lepers, so people sent them to live on the outskirts of the village. Although they had other lepers for company, they could no longer mix with their own family and friends. There was no cure. People suspected of having the disease would be sent away and it was difficult to get permission to return. However, if your skin problem turned out not to be permanent and you recovered, you could show yourself to a priest and get permission to mix in society again.

You could pause at the mid-point in the story and ask the children to 'hot-seat' the characters. What would you have done if you had been one of the lepers walking away and realized that your skin had been healed? Rushed home in excitement? Rushed to find a priest to prove you were cured? Gone back to Jesus? (You could use the garden cane thought bubble as a prop here.)

Jesus seemed a bit annoyed that only one of the men came back to say 'thank you' to him, and that person was the one least expected to do so, as he was not one of God's people (the Jewish people). He was from the area over the border in Samaria, where people lived in a different way and didn't stick to all the rules that the Jewish religion laid down for worship.

Suggestions for songs

- Thank you, Lord (*Come and Praise* 32) (Words could be adapted to 'mums and dads', 'all our friends' and so on
- Count your blessings (*Songs for Every Assembly*—Out of the Ark)
- Thank you, Jesus, thank you, Lord, for loving me (*Kidsource* 313)

Suggested prayer

Thank you, Father God, that you love us. Thank you, too, for all our family and friends who care for us. Help us to remember to say 'thank you' to them whenever we get the chance, so that they know how grateful we are for all their help. Amen

For quiet reflection, tease out what we can learn from the story about being grateful and saying so. Guide the children using your own words, or the following suggestion.

Picture in your mind some of the people who help you, at home and in school… Think of what they do to help… Picture yourself saying 'thank you' to them… In the quiet now, say 'thank you' to God for them… Now remember to thank them when you see them next… You could even give yourself a challenge to say ten 'thank you's today.

All Saints Day

All Saints

This assembly could be used as an introduction to a series on saints, or at the time of All Saints Day itself. It tries to answer the question, 'What is a saint?' It is a slightly longer assembly as it needs to establish some key ideas about saints, which can be expanded upon later. Alternatively, the assembly could be shortened or spread over two days.

Bible links

Jesus went off to a mountain to pray, and he spent the whole night there. The next morning he called his disciples together and chose twelve of them to be his apostles. One was Simon, and Jesus named him Peter. Another was Andrew, Peter's brother. There were also James, John, Philip, Bartholomew, Matthew, Thomas, and James the son of Alphaeus. The rest of the apostles were Simon, known as the Eager One, Jude, who was the son of James, and Judas Iscariot, who later betrayed Jesus.

LUKE 6:12–16

Key background information for the teacher

In the church calendar, All Saints is celebrated on 1 November, followed the next day by All Souls, remembering all Christians who have died. Significant saints have particular days on which their actions are remembered, which are scattered across the year. Some of the saints with special days in the autumn have assemblies based on them in this book.

A good place to start when thinking about saints is with the people whom Jesus chose as his friends and trained to carry on with his work. Some are listed among the twelve apostles, while others are known to us through the record of their lives in the Bible. Well-known biblical saints include the four Gospel writers, Matthew, Mark, Luke and John, and key figures such as Mary the mother of Jesus, and the apostle Paul.

The Church added to this list later with names of people who became well known for serving others and trying to show God's love, or fighting against injustice and helping people in need.

In his writings, Paul often refers to God's people as 'saints' because they have chosen to follow the teaching of Jesus, and this makes their outlook on life different from that of other people. They have lives filled with God's love and God's Spirit.

Suggestions for visual aids and resources

⚙ A painting of a saint from a gallery, complete with halo
⚙ A list of saints as an example
⚙ The names Matthew and Luke on card
⚙ A picture of Mother Teresa
⚙ A baby name book (for names referenced to saints)
⚙ The letters S A I N T, each on a separate A4 card

Ideas for exploring the theme

Have the letters of the word SAINT ready on cards. Ask quiz questions that will provide you with the five letters (in the wrong order), and then ask if anyone can reshuffle the letters to form a word. You are likely to get the words ANTS, SATIN or STAIN, but someone should hit on the word SAINT before long.

Here are some possible quiz questions to find the letters. You can adapt them to the age group of the audience.

- Sing a song of... (**S**ixpence)
- Almond and Brazil are types of what? (**N**ut)
- A house of ice (**I**gloo)
- God's heavenly messengers (**A**ngels)
- A shape with three sides (**T**riangle)

Then use the background information above and the following ideas to explain (at a level appropriate to your audience) what the word 'saint' means to different people. Show a list of saints' names or read some out. Do the children recognize any of these names? Does anyone have the same name as one of the saints' names?

Famous saints were often pictured in classical art with a halo (a bright circular glow around the head) to show that they were special to God. (People who were viewed as especially holy but were still alive were sometimes pictured with square halos.)

Someone often regarded as a modern-day saint is Mother Teresa of Calcutta. Calcutta is an overcrowded Indian city, well known for its poverty. Mother Teresa worked tirelessly there with people who were homeless, orphaned or dying. (A picture of her would be helpful, especially one that could be copied on to an OHP or whiteboard.) You can look up what she did on websites or in books.

There are days throughout the year when individual saints are remembered. During the autumn we particularly remember St Matthew, St Luke, St Francis, St Andrew and St Nicholas, and we mark All Saints Day on 1 November (followed by a remembrance festival called All Souls, when people remember family and friends who have died, and thank God for them).

Today we'll learn a little about St Matthew and St Luke. (We learn more about them in their own special assemblies, and about other saints in other assemblies.) Matthew is traditionally remembered on 21 September and Luke on 18 October. (You could have these two names on cards so that children can see them—there may be children with these names who could hold the cards up.) Matthew and Luke wrote two of the books in the New Testament part of the Bible, which tell us what they knew about the life of Jesus and what he did and said. Matthew wrote his book to help explain to the Jewish people of his day why Jesus was important, and Luke's book was written to show that the message of God's love would be important for the whole world.

There are further ideas on saints on pages 139–142, both for use in a class assembly and linked to other areas of the curriculum. The children could be challenged to write their own acrostic or to perform a rhyming poem that speaks about each believer being a saint. These ideas could, of course, be used to extend the original assembly if enough preparation time is available.

Suggestions for songs

☉ O when the saints go marching in (*Junior Praise* 195)
☉ When I needed a neighbour (*Come and Praise* 65)
☉ He's got the whole world in his hand (*Come and Praise* 19)
☉ Jesus' love is very wonderful (*Kidsource* 208)
☉ One more step (*Come and Praise* 47)

Suggested prayer

Thank you, Lord God, for the people who set us good examples of how to behave and show your love to others. Help us, too, to be quick to help and to speak words of kindness. Thank you for the people who wrote down Jesus' words so that we can all learn from what he said and did. Amen

✛

All Saints Day

<Assembly 2>

Gideon, the reluctant hero

In this assembly we explore the theme of potential. Christians believe that every Christian is a 'saint in the making'. We are in training for God's team and he is the coach. The story of Gideon shows that God is interested in developing the skills he has given us and helping us to develop new ones. Gideon was something of a reluctant hero, even though he knew that God was asking him to lead. He was a 'saint in the making' and only later was he recognized as a hero. Even then, he surely must have given the credit for his victories to the God who inspired him.

Still today, God wants his people to rely on him for help and guidance, not just on their own abilities. The assembly makes the point that God can use anyone who puts himself or herself at his disposal. (In this respect, this assembly links well to the assembly about 'Treasure in clay pots' on page 94.) With us, God not only sees a seed, but also the 'tree' we will become.

Bible links

Then the Lord himself said, 'Gideon, you will be strong, because I am giving you the power to rescue Israel from the Midianites.' Gideon replied, 'But how can I rescue Israel? My clan is the weakest one in Manasseh, and everyone in my family is more important than I am.' 'Gideon,' the Lord answered, 'you can rescue Israel because I am going to help you!'

JUDGES 6:14–16a

Key background information for the teacher

Gideon was one of the judges of Israel. The judges were national heroes in the period between the invasion of Canaan and the establishment of the monarchy. Most of them were military leaders, although Gideon was rather a reluctant one. The most famous is probably Samson. All the stories in the book of Judges remind us that the survival of Israel depended on being loyal to God. Conversely, disloyalty led to disaster, although God was always ready to rescue his people if they repented and once again promised to follow his ways.

Suggestions for visual aids and resources

- ✪ A lantern
- ✪ A trumpet
- ✪ Noisy percussion instruments
- ✪ An acorn
- ✪ Any seed and its fruit

Ideas for exploring the theme

Ask the children if they have ever been asked to do a job that they knew they would find hard—for example, winning a difficult race, taking part in a sports tournament against stiff opposition, or learning a certain times table. Explain that the story you are going to look at today is about someone who thought God was asking him to do the impossible, but in the end, after lots of excuses, he found that with God's help it was possible. He learnt an important lesson about trusting God for help. He was very much a trainee follower but he learned to rely on God. We might call him a 'saint in the making'. God seemed to know him better than he knew himself.

Prepare some actions with the children so that they can join in with the story as it is told. Whenever they hear the words 'worried', 'afraid' or 'weak', they should put their fingernails in their mouth. Whenever they hear the words 'soldier' or 'army', they salute. Whenever they hear the word 'God', they punch a fist into the air.

Practise the reaction to the words a little first. You will also need to prepare in advance if you want to use musical instruments to create an outburst of noise in the story.

Now read the story. The rather reluctant hero is Gideon.

Gideon was certainly **worried**. His people, the Israelites, had been attacked over and over again by the **army** of the Midianites. One day at work he had a visitor. 'You're a great **soldier**, Gideon,' the man said. Gideon laughed, because he thought that **God** had forgotten about them, and he told the man so, but the man replied, 'Oh no he hasn't, and he's going to send you into battle as the leader of his **army** to fight the enemy!'

Gideon realized that this was no ordinary man who had come to visit him, but an angel with a message from **God**. 'I'm too **afraid** to do it,' he said. 'I'm too **weak** to lead the **army**. Can't somebody else do it?' The angel just calmly repeated that Gideon was the one **God** had chosen to be in charge of the **army**, and that he should trust **God** for the help he needed.'

Gideon set about gathering all the **soldiers** who lived in the land. There were thousands of them. 'Great!' thought

Gideon. 'With such a large **army**, we stand a really good chance of winning.' But **God** had other ideas and wanted to make a point to Gideon. 'I want everyone to know that it is because I am on your side that you are going to win, not because of your cleverness or the size of the **army**!' he said. He told Gideon to send most of the **soldiers** home. Gideon was left with just 300 of the best **soldiers**.

It wasn't surprising that Gideon didn't sleep well that night. He was **worried** because there were thousands of Midianite **soldiers** camped nearby, no doubt planning their attack. **God** knew that he was **worried**, so he put the idea into Gideon's mind of creeping into the enemy camp to listen to their conversations. What a surprise! Gideon heard his enemies talking about how **God** was with the Israelites, and how **worried** they all were about the next battle. Now Gideon felt more certain that **God** was going to help them win, and he began to plan his own **army's** attack. He had a bright idea after finding it so easy to creep into the Midianite camp.

Gideon woke up his **soldiers** and told each of them to pick up a water jar and cover their torch with it. As well as putting on swords, they should carry something to make a lot of noise, such as a ram's horn trumpet. *(At this point, if you are using musical instruments, get the children to pick them up quietly.)* He explained about his visit to the enemy camp and how he knew that the **soldiers** of the enemy were **afraid** of the Israelites because **God** was with them!

Their approach to the enemy was silent, but then they erupted into a frenzy of noise and fighting as they smashed the jars and created as much noise as they could. *(Get the children to make as loud a noise as possible with their instruments.)* The enemy had no idea what was happening and their **soldiers** were very **afraid**. They ran off as fast as their legs would carry them, back towards their own towns. It was an easy victory for the Israelite **army**, who knew that it was **God** who had helped Gideon to win. Gideon felt a little foolish that he had been reluctant to fight, but so glad that he was now being treated as a hero by his **army**, all because he had trusted **God**!

What do you think Gideon told his troops when they were about to go into battle? You could use a speech bubble on a stick and ask someone to speak his words: for example, 'I trust God to help us, so follow me!' There is a thought bubble template on page 173.

Suggestions for songs

- ✪ For all the saints (a traditional hymn, which can be shortened as required) (*Hymns Old and New* 134)
- ✪ Colours of day (*Come and Praise* 55)
- ✪ For I'm building a people of power (*Kidsource* 61)

Suggested prayer

Thank you, Lord God, for the example of Gideon, who trusted you for help and guidance. We pray that the leaders of our country and our churches will trust you in the same way. Thank you that you know the skills and even the hidden talents of each one of us. Help us to be ready to use them for you and to serve others. Amen

Guy Fawkes

Assembly 1

Remember, remember

This assembly presents a simple version of the historical background to Guy Fawkes, who is an unlikely hero to celebrate. He and his fellow conspirators were certainly men of great conviction, who decided to act on it, although many people would consider their actions misplaced. This is an opportunity to give children a flavour of the events, but also to consider what sort of people we follow as our heroes and why.

Bible link

Keep your minds on whatever is true, pure, right, holy, friendly, and proper. Don't ever stop thinking about what is truly worthwhile and worthy of praise.

PHILIPPIANS 4:8

Key background information for the teacher

In 1605, Guy Fawkes (also known as Guido) and a group of conspirators attempted to blow up the Houses of Parliament while the king was inside.

After Queen Elizabeth I died in 1603, Catholic Christians in

England, who had had a rough time in the later part of her reign, hoped that her successor, King James I, would allow them to worship in their own way. This turned out not to be the case, and a group of angry young men decided that the only answer was violence. They saw a chance to blow up the Houses of Parliament while the king was visiting, and hoped that the king and the Members of Parliament, who were making life difficult for the Catholics, would die in the explosion. Today, such people would most probably be called terrorists or freedom fighters.

Before the men were able to carry out their plan, however, they were caught, tortured and put to death. Guy was captured around midnight on 4 November. On 5 November, the Privy Council allowed him to be tortured until he admitted—two days later—that the plan had been to blow up Parliament and release prisoners such as Sir Walter Raleigh from the Tower of London.

How were the conspirators found out? It may be that some of them had second thoughts, and someone may have betrayed the others by letting the king's men know of the plot, but this is uncertain. There may just have been a security patrol that did its job well and spotted the gunpowder. But the most likely solution, according to researchers, is that Thomas Tresham (a friend of the conspirators who knew the plot) wrote to friends advising them not to attend Parliament, and this is how word reached the authorities.

We have traditionally celebrated Guy Fawkes' failure by letting off fireworks and burning an effigy of a 'guy'. Some people naturally wonder whether celebrating Guy Fawkes' execution, or honouring his attempt to do away with the government, is a good idea.

Suggestions for visual aids and resources

✪ A copy of 'Remember, Remember' (see Worksheet 1, which can be downloaded free of charge from the 'Books and resources' section of the website www.barnabasinschools.org.uk)

✪ An OHT of the famous picture of the conspirators. (This image is easily obtained through www.google.com: search Images for Guy Fawkes.)

✪ Objects linked to fictional superheroes such as Batman, or objects linked to a lighthouse, the coastguard or the RNLI (optional)

Ideas for exploring the theme

You could open the assembly with a general song or play a starter game on a remembering theme, such as Kim's game, where you display some objects on a tray and then remove one before revealing the selection again to see if children can spot what has been removed. You could then interview children about how far back into their childhood they can remember. (See page 75 for other ideas about remembering.)

Explain that in our history lessons we usually remember famous people who did brave or exciting things—explorers like Christopher Columbus, people who have broken records, or saints who lived holy lives, like St Francis (you could substitute people known to the children or part of recent topics). Often, in our assemblies we remember Jesus for his exciting teaching and actions. For Christians, he is a hero.

What is a hero? Someone who comes to the rescue, or fights for what is right; someone who thinks of others and helps them. Heroes might be fictional characters like Superman, or real-life people, such as lifeboat rescue teams and people who raise lots of money for charity and save lives in such ways. (You could have visual aids such as a cape, Batman mask, Spiderman outfit or information on charities such as the RNLI.)

This makes it all the more unusual that, at this time of the year, we honour England's most notorious traitor. People seem to like a villain, especially one who gets caught! (Another example is Dick Turpin.) It's strange, though, that many years after Guy Fawkes' death, fireworks are still set off, bonfires are lit, and guys made and burnt.

You could show the children an OHT of the well-known print of the conspirators. In the picture, Guy is third from the right.

Below is a famous rhyme about Guy Fawkes, the first part of which is known by children even today. Read out the poem. Can anyone spot the word ending that doesn't sound right? Some words have changed over time!

Remember, remember the fifth of November.
Gunpowder, treason and plot.
I see no reason why gunpowder treason
Should ever be forgot!
Guy Fawkes Guy, 'twas his intent
To blow up king and parliament.
Three score barrels were laid below
To prove old England's overthrow.
By God's mercy he was catched
With a dark lantern and lighted match.
Holler boys, holler boys, let the bells ring,
Holler boys, holler boys, God save the king.

Suggestions for songs

- Thank you, Lord, for this new day (*Come and Praise* 32)
- One more step (*Come and Praise* 47)
- Dear Lord and Father of mankind (*Hymns Old and New* 106)
- Fight the good fight (*Hymns Old and New* 128)

Suggested prayer

Sometimes it can be useful to explain to children what you are going to pray about, so that they can be encouraged to listen and to respond with the 'Amen' if they agree with the prayer. Today's prayer reminds us to think carefully about whom we follow as our examples.

Dear God, today, as we think about the story of Guy Fawkes, help us to think of others rather than ourselves and to fight for what is pleasing to you. Help us to choose wisely the people we follow as our heroes. Amen

Guy Fawkes

(Assembly 2)

Remember the firework safety code

This is one of four assemblies on the theme of remembering, embracing the season of firework parties and national Remembrance. This assembly focuses on accepting recommended safety advice and not taking risks with fireworks.

Bible links

Fools think they know what is best, but a sensible person listens to advice.

PROVERBS 12:15

Key background information for the teacher

Despite the popularity of local group displays of fireworks, there are still too many children and young adults injured by fireworks each year, almost all in people's gardens or in the street as people disregard safety advice. Try not to appear too 'preachy' in this assembly, but do show your pastoral care, emphasizing that you don't want anybody in school to get injured in the next few days. Try to make it visual, perhaps by using the gloves and buckets of water and sand (see below).

Suggestions for visual aids and resources

⊙ A firework safety code—either the one printed below or one copied from the side of a box of fireworks or packet of sparklers. (Some individual fireworks, such as sparklers, or the instructions on a box of mixed fireworks would be useful to show the children.)
⊙ A pair of gloves and two buckets, one containing water and the other sand
⊙ Handel's *Music for the Royal Fireworks*

Ideas for exploring the theme

You could begin by asking the children why they think you have brought two buckets to assembly. They will probably guess quickly that there is a link to fireworks. If not, you could show a packet of fireworks. Talk through the way that sparklers in particular are a danger to many children, as they stay very hot even after they seem to have gone out. A bucket of either sand or water can be a useful place to put them after use. Wearing gloves offers some protection from the sparks but not from direct contact with the metal part that is heated.

Ask how many of the children will be remembering Guy Fawkes and Bonfire Night with fireworks. Many of them will go to big organized displays, but it may be that they will have a few fireworks at home, set off by an adult. Even holding sparklers can be dangerous unless you follow the safety rules.

Our keyword for this group of assemblies is 'remember'. We would do well to remember our safety rules at this time of the year, with so many fireworks being set off. The government has produced a safety leaflet to help keep everyone safe, and safety instructions can also be found on a box of fireworks or packet of sparklers.

NB: The full advice sheet could be distributed to staff so that they can reinforce the message of the assembly in a PSHE lesson or classroom discussion to follow. The Department of Trade and Industry website (www.dti.gov.uk/fireworks) has a section for teachers and access to resources online—well worth a look!

Here is an example of the information and instructions on the side of a packet of sparklers:

- Keep sparklers in safe hands.
- Sparklers injure more people than any other fireworks.
- Many of the victims are children under five.

Explain that fireworks are fantastic for celebrating and can be a great way to get together with friends, family or the local people in your community, but you don't want anyone to get hurt and come back to school bandaged up. The Bible doesn't have a special message in it about fireworks! What it does have are lots of wise sayings about following sensible advice (see the Bible links on page 68). Please be very safe over the next few days and remember not to take risks with fireworks.

To end the assembly, play Handel's *Music for the Royal Fireworks*. Explain that the music was written by George Frederick Handel and performed in Green Park in London on 27 April 1749 in the presence of King George II.

Suggestions for songs

- Lead us, heavenly Father, lead us (*Hymns Old and New* 293)
- This is the day that the Lord has made (*Kidsource* 341)
- Come on and celebrate (*Kidsource* 34)

Suggested prayer

Father God, thank you for the fun celebrations at this time of year when we can get together with family and friends. Please keep all those who are organizing firework parties safe. Amen

Here is an easy checklist to keep you safe this year.

Before the display

✓ Check that the fireworks you buy are suitable for the size of your garden and conform to British Standards (BS 7114; 1988).

✓ Ensure that your display area is free from hazards.

✓ Do not tamper with fireworks.

✓ Read the instructions in daylight.

✓ Warn neighbours, especially the elderly and those with animals, about your display.

✓ One person—clearly identified—should be responsible for the fireworks.

Things you will need on the night

✓ Metal box, with a lid for storage.

✓ Torch for checking instructions.

✓ Bucket of water.

✓ Protective hat, eye protection and gloves.

✓ First Aid kit.

✓ Bucket of soft earth to stick fireworks in.

✓ A board for flat-bottomed fireworks.

✓ Suitable supports for Catherine wheels.

✓ Proper launchers for rockets.

During the display

✓ Light fireworks at arm's length with a taper.

✓ Stand well back.

✓ Never go back to a lit firework.

✓ Keep storage box closed between use.

✓ Keep children under control.

Reproduced with permission from *Assemblies for Autumn Festivals* published by BRF 2007 (1 84101 459 1)

www.barnabasinschools.org.uk

After the display

✓ Use tongs or gloves to collect spent fireworks.
✓ Next morning, check again and remove firework debris.

Sparklers

✓ Unsuitable for children under five.
✓ Light one at a time.
✓ Hold at arm's length.
✓ Wear gloves when holding sparklers.
✓ Put used sparklers, hot end down, into a bucket of sand or water.

Bonfires

✓ Organize properly.
✓ Should be at least 18 metres (60 feet) away from houses, trees, hedges, fences or sheds.
✓ Before lighting, check for animals and children.
✓ Use domestic firelighters.
✓ Never use petrol, paraffin or other flammable liquids.
✓ Never put used fireworks, aerosols, foam-filled furniture, batteries, tins of paint or tyres on a bonfire.

EXTRACTS TAKEN FROM DTI LEAFLET

Reproduced with permission from *Assemblies for Autumn Festivals* published by BRF 2007 (1 84101 459 1)
www.barnabasinschools.org.uk

Remembrance

Remembrance

The aim of this assembly is for the children to appreciate how important remembering is for us, as individuals and as a country. Part of the purpose is to explain why people wear a poppy at this time of year and how the money raised by donation is used. It will also prepare children for any act of remembrance to be held in school on 11 November, or at local churches or memorials on a Sunday close to this date. It may be that some of the children belong to Guides, Brownies, Scouts, Cubs or Boys' Brigade and have plans to attend a war memorial service in the coming few days, so the assembly could also help prepare them for this ceremony. Children who have attended remembrance services in the past could be invited in the assembly to explain to other children what happens.

The other assembly in this pair is a format for an act of remembrance (see pp. 78–80). It may be appropriate to learn one of the suggested songs on page 76 so that you can sing it as part of the act of remembrance. The format of the act could be explained at the end of this assembly or in a short practice beforehand.

Bible links

We know what love is because Jesus gave his life for us. That's why we must give our lives for each other. If we have all we need and see one of our own people in need, we must have pity on that person, or else we cannot say we love God.

1 JOHN 3:16–17

Key background information for the teacher

The money donated for poppies makes up part of the Earl Haig Fund. This fund is used in a wide variety of ways to alleviate the suffering and difficulties both of those involved in war and of their dependants. The collections are organized by the Royal British Legion, who also take responsibility for many of the national Remembrance celebrations. It is well worth using the Internet to research the current work of the RBL and the focus of this year's poppy collections. Typically, money is used to enable people to be visited at home or in hospital, paying war pensions, paying for holiday homes or helping people to visit war graves, to give just a few examples.

The poppy is a symbol and can therefore convey layers of meaning. Understandings can vary from person to person. The poppy is used to raise money for the survivors and the bereaved because the fields in France that had been so radically disturbed by the fighting in World War I were noted for their displays of poppies. Poppy seed is an excellent survivor, therefore symbolizing new life, a fresh start and survival.

Care should be taken to check whether any child in school has had a recent bereavement. Talking about how tokens of remembrance remind us of special people who have died can be a positive benefit, but it should be handled sensitively and the focus quickly returned to remembrance of those lost in war. For children who have family members in the armed services, this can have a very present resonance.

Suggestions for visual aids and resources

- A poppy
- Information about the work of the Royal British Legion, printed for schools or on the Internet
- Suitable music such as William Walton's *Spitfire Prelude and Fugue*, Eric Coates' *Dambusters March*, or something more reflective such as 'Nimrod' from Edward Elgar's *Enigma Variations*
- The 'Remember' song, which can be downloaded free of charge from the 'Books and resources' section of the *Barnabas* website, www.barnabasinschools.org.uk

Ideas for exploring the theme

Suggest that there are special times in the year when we stop to remember important occasions. Ask children for suggestions—birthdays, anniversaries, Guy Fawkes, the birth of Jesus and so on.

We do different things to remember different occasions. Ask children to identify what special things we might use to help us to remember the reason for the occasion—for example, fireworks for Guy Fawkes; presents, stars and carols at Christmas; cards for birthdays and anniversaries.

Ask the children how good they are at remembering. For example, can they remember what they had for lunch yesterday or last Saturday? What presents did they get for their last birthday? It's often good if we have something to help us remember—a bit like making a list when we go shopping. Talk about a favourite photo or a souvenir from an enjoyable holiday.

If appropriate, you could talk about memories of someone who has died. This needs care if there has been a recent bereavement, but can also be a positive experience if handled well. People often find that it helps to keep some special mementoes in an album or a box. Such objects help us to remember times, places and people. We can then look back and be thankful for those special people and times.

Use the poppy now to explain how it helps us to remember those who have served their country and been injured or killed in wars. The soldiers who fought in wars were ordinary people who showed great courage in fighting for what they believed to be right, being unselfish to help others. They have made it possible for us to have the freedom to make our own laws and decisions as a country. You can relate the poppy specifically to World War I, when the poppies grew on the ground that had been disturbed by heavy fighting, but you can also link it to more recent conflicts such as World War II, the Falklands War, Northern Ireland, the Gulf War, Iraq or wherever people have served our country to fight or act as peacekeepers.

If you have information abut the Royal British Legion and how the 'poppy money' (the Earl Haig Fund) is used (for example, visiting people at home or in hospital, paying war pensions, paying for holiday homes, helping people to visit war graves and so on), this could be shared now.

Explain what happens on 11 November and how you intend to mark the occasion in school. You may choose to use special music or poems about war, or learn a song.

Suggestions for songs

❂ Make me a channel of your peace (*Come and Praise* 147)
❂ Remember (see Worksheet 2, which can be downloaded free of charge from the 'Books and resources' section of the *Barnabas* website, www.barnabasinschools.org.uk)
❂ We will remember (*Songs for Every Occasion*—Out of the Ark CD series)

You could practise any song or hymn that you intend to use for your act of remembrance, including those suggested above. CD music for this assembly could include something with a war-time association, such as a song sung by soldiers or a war-time singer such as Vera Lynn, or perhaps a march such as William Walton's *Spitfire Prelude and Fugue* or Eric Coates' *Dambusters March*. Alternatively, it may seem more appropriate to play something more reflective, such as 'Nimrod' from Edward Elgar's *Enigma Variations*.

Suggested prayer

Father God, we remember with thanks all the people who were injured or died in wars, all who risked their lives in the Air Force, Navy or Army, or as fire-fighters, ambulance drivers, doctors and nurses. Thank you for their courage and dedication to duty. Thank you for all those who look after the injured, who visit them at home or look after them in British Legion homes. Amen

Assembly 2

An act of remembrance for Remembrance Day

This act of remembrance can be used with the whole school on 11 November at 11.00 am. If you wish to use the song 'Remember', it should be taught in advance so that the assembly can flow uninterrupted. It can be downloaded from the 'Books and resources' section of the website www.barnabasinschools.org.uk (Worksheet 2). Alternatively, someone could read the words of the song as a poem. The service sheet should be copied so that everyone can see it (on OHP, paper copies or projected on to a whiteboard). Both the modern and traditional versions of the Lord's Prayer are given below, so feel free to use whichever words are more familiar to the children.

The service can stand alone or could follow an assembly on Remembrance (see pp. 73–77). If you would like to extend the act of remembrance, the responses in the Iona worship book *A Service for Justice and Peace*, from The Iona Community (published by Wild Goose Publications), are very fitting.

Suggestions for visual aids and resources

○ A large white candle
○ Candle lighter or matches

An act of remembrance

Lighting the candle

We light this candle to show that there are many dark places in the world that need light. We light this candle to show that we believe there is hope.

Song or poem: Remember

What are your feelings when you think of the war?
What do you think all the fighting was for?
Many years later we wear poppies with pride
As we remember with thanks all the people who died—
Those who made sacrifices to make sure we'd be free
To decide for ourselves how our future should be.
May we be peacemakers, but never forget
Those on whose lives the sun has now set.

(Repeat last line if you are singing the song.)

Words of remembrance

Leader: They shall not grow old as we that are left grow old;
Age shall not weary them, nor the years condemn.
At the going down of the sun and in the morning
We will remember them.

All: We will remember them.

(Silence is kept)

The Lord's Prayer

Traditional version

Our Father, who art in heaven,
Hallowed be thy name;
Thy kingdom come,
Thy will be done,
On earth as it is in heaven.
Give us this day our daily bread
And forgive us our trespasses,
As we forgive those who trespass against us.
And lead us not into temptation,
But deliver us from evil;
For thine is the kingdom, the power and the glory,
For ever and ever.
Amen

The Lord's Prayer

Modern version

Our Father in heaven,
Hallowed be your name,
Your kingdom come,
your will be done,
on earth as in heaven.
Give us today our daily bread.
Forgive us our sins
as we forgive those who sin against us.
Lead us not into temptation,
but deliver us from evil.
For the kingdom, the power and the glory are yours
Now and for ever.
Amen

Christ the King

⟨ **Assembly 1** ⟩

The servant king

This assembly focuses on how Jesus fits into a long tradition of kings featured in the Bible—although he is clearly different, not only because he is God's Son, but also because of the type of king he is.

Bible links

One day [the Lord] said, 'Samuel... Put some olive oil in a small container and go and visit a man named Jesse, who lives in Bethlehem. I have chosen one of his sons to be my king.' ... Jesse sent all seven of his sons over to Samuel. Finally, Samuel said, 'Jesse, the Lord hasn't chosen any of these young men. Do you have any more sons?' 'Yes,' Jesse answered. 'My youngest son David is out taking care of the sheep.' 'Send for him!' Samuel said. 'We won't start the ceremony until he gets here.' Jesse sent for David. He was a healthy, good-looking boy with a sparkle in his eyes. As soon as David came, the Lord told Samuel, 'He's the one! Get up and pour the olive oil on his head.' Samuel poured the oil on David's head while his brothers watched. At that moment, the Spirit of the Lord took control of David and stayed with him from then on.

1 SAMUEL 16:1 and 10–13

Jesus said, 'I am the good shepherd. I know my sheep, and they know me.'
JOHN 10:14

The next day a large crowd was in Jerusalem for Passover. When they heard that Jesus was coming for the festival, they took palm branches and went out to greet him… Jesus found a donkey and rode on it, just as the Scriptures say.
JOHN 12:12–14

Everyone in Jerusalem, celebrate and shout! Your king has won a victory, and he is coming to you. He is humble and rides on a donkey; he comes on the colt of a donkey.
ZECHARIAH 9:9

Pilate ordered the charge against Jesus to be written on a board and put above the cross. It read, 'Jesus of Nazareth, King of the Jews'.
JOHN 19:19

Christ was truly God. But he did not try to remain equal with God. Instead he gave up everything and became a slave, when he became like one of us. Christ was humble. He obeyed God and even died on a cross. Then God gave Christ the highest place and honoured his name above all others. So at the name of Jesus everyone will bow down, those in heaven, on earth, and under the earth. And to the glory of God the Father everyone will openly agree, 'Jesus Christ is Lord!'
PHILIPPIANS 2:6–11

Key background information for the teacher

Throughout the Bible God is regarded as supreme, but in the Old Testament we have a record of how he agreed to allow his people to be ruled by kings under his command. God chose the kings of Israel through his prophets, and Jesus was recognized by many as God's appointed king, his anointed leader. However, many people were surprised to find that Jesus was not the sort of king they were expecting (one who would free them from the political rule of the Romans), even though there are clearly strong links back to his ancestor, King David, the 'shepherd king'.

In pictures of kings and queens, people are often shown bowing and the monarch is seen holding a symbol of power, such as a sceptre, and an orb, showing control of the world. A king is also in charge of the army and is willing to die for his people. In religious art, Jesus is typically pictured wearing two sorts of crowns, an archetypal kingly jewelled crown and one made of thorns, reminding us how the soldiers at his crucifixion mocked him because he had spoken about having his own kingdom and yet was condemned to death.

During Advent, Christians remember that Jesus said he would return to the world one day and, at his second coming, there would be no doubt in people's minds about who he is. Advent is a time when Christians think about preparing for Jesus' return. They ask themselves the question, 'How can I best get ready?' We can think about it in terms of getting ready for the arrival of a VIP, and then consider how we would get ready to welcome Jesus when he returns. Would we behave any differently? How would we welcome him? Would it be the same as on Palm Sunday?

Suggestions for visual aids and resources

❂ A cardboard crown
❂ A picture of a king or queen holding an orb and sceptre
❂ A list of the kings and queens of England
❂ A chair with arms draped in fine (velvet) cloth
❂ A picture of a traditional crown alongside a crown of thorns

Ideas for exploring the theme

Ask if anyone knows the names of any of the kings or queens of England, or play 'Who am I?' and pretend to be a particular king, such as Henry VIII. See if children can guess who you are within a set number of guesses. Can children name any kings from the Bible? (David, Solomon and Nebuchadnezzar are perhaps the most famous.)

To develop the theme, explain how, in Bible times, a new king was anointed by having oil poured over his head. This anointing was often done by one of God's prophets, such as Samuel, who chose David the shepherd boy to be the next king after Saul. There is a musical by Roger Jones, called *David*, which has a song about this: you might like to play part of it to the children (see page 174 for details.) Alternatively, you could invite someone to come out and be treated like a king. Give them a cardboard crown and have 'servants' bowing and running errands for favourite drinks and so on. Give the 'king' symbols of power, such as new laws to be signed.

Explain that at this time of the year Christians celebrate Jesus as Christ the King. Some churches are dedicated to Christ the King, or Christ the Cornerstone. There may be a church with this type of dedication in your area.

Jesus was given many titles, some chosen by himself and some by others—for example, Messiah, Christ, the Good Shepherd, King of the Jews and so on. Christians today often think of Jesus as the 'servant king', a name that acknowledges who they believe Jesus to be, but also speaks of the way Jesus behaved towards others. God had promised that he would send his people a good king whose kingdom would last for ever. However, God's new king would not be the kind of king who bosses everyone around or makes the people give him money (as in some folk tales). God's king would be more like a shepherd who knows each of his sheep individually and protects and cares for them.

Ask children to suggest in what ways Jesus was like a king—for example, he was a leader, a role model and someone who showed God's love. (You could write suggestions around a picture of a crown that has Jesus' name round the rim.) Jesus also talked about God's kingdom and his own authority within that kingdom. When Jesus arrived in Jerusalem on Palm Sunday, he behaved like a king to show people that he wanted to create a rule of love and respect in people's lives.

This action fulfilled what was predicted in Zechariah 9:9 (see 'Bible links' above). There is also a passage in Paul's letter to the Philippians that speaks of how Jesus died, rose again and is now acknowledged as king in the sense that 'at the name of Jesus everyone will bow down' (see 'Bible links' above).

Anyone can ask to become part of God's kingdom if they believe in Jesus, the Son of God who was born in a stable, died on a cross and came back to life again. God's kingdom is a kingdom of love, peace and forgiveness.

Suggestions for songs

- He's got the whole world in his hands (*Come and Praise* 19)
- Who's the king of the jungle? (*Kidsource* 388)
- The servant king (*Kidsource* 62)
- King of kings and Lord of lords (can be sung as a round) (*The Source* 307)
- The King of Love my shepherd is (*Come and Praise* 54)
- At the name of Jesus (*Come and Praise* 58)

You could also play William Walton's *Crown Imperial* or *Orb and Sceptre*, any music used at a coronation, or *David*, a musical by Roger Jones.

Suggested prayer

Thank you, Jesus, that you showed us how a good king should behave, serving others and looking after his people just like a shepherd looks after his sheep. Please help all those in charge of the countries of this world, whether they are kings, queens, presidents or prime ministers. Give them the wisdom they need to make the right decisions so that our world might become a safer and more caring place. Help us to remember that God's kingdom is based on love, peace and forgiveness. Amen

Christ the King

Assembly 2

The kingdom of peace

The prophet Isaiah told of a time when a special king would come to bring peace. He used a word-picture of contrasting animals who would normally be enemies but live in harmony in God's kingdom, to reinforce his message.

Bible links

Leopards will lie down with young goats, and wolves will rest with lambs. Calves and lions will eat together and be cared for by little children. Cows and bears will share the same pasture; their young will rest side by side. Lions and oxen will both eat straw.
ISAIAH 11:6–7

Key background information for the teacher

By the time Jesus was born, people had high expectations of the coming Messiah. There are many prophecies in what we now know as the Old Testament predicting the nature of God's coming king. It would have been natural for a country under Roman rule to hope for a warrior who would release God's people from oppression, but a closer reading of the different texts points more to the role of a prophet, re-establishing a right relationship with God in people's hearts—a leader who would change attitudes. The passage from Isaiah (see 'Bible links' above) stands at the heart of this understanding, with its theme of peace.

Christians believe that Jesus is the awaited king, whose mission was to fight evil and bring in an era of peace and justice. When God's kingdom, or rule, comes, surprising things happen. Relationships can be reformed—most obviously our relationship with God (symbolized in baptism), but the way we respond to other people will also be different as God changes us.

Suggestions for visual aids and resources

✪ Match the Pairs (see Worksheet 3, which can be downloaded free of charge from the 'Books and resources' section of the *Barnabas* website, www.barnabasinschools.org.uk). This could also be done with two made-up lists on an OHT, which children can link together with lines (the sort of thing children are used to in their SATs tests). If you make up your own lists, include pairs that don't fit quite so well.

Ideas for exploring the theme

Use the prepared cards or OHT to do some sorting and matching. Can the children think of other ridiculous or uncomfortable combinations (for example, cat and mouse)? Now read the words from Isaiah 11 about the kingdom of peace (see 'Bible links' above). You could ask a child to prepare this reading. Explain that the prophet Isaiah spoke to people around 600 years before Jesus was born, about how God wanted them to live and about God's plans for the future. His idea was that God's special king would come to bring peace. Isaiah used the idea of contrasting animals to explain how different God wanted the world to be, with everyone living together in peace rather than arguing and fighting. Isaiah wanted this peace and harmony in his own time but even more so in the future, when people would listen to God's special messenger, his king, and would follow his ways more and more.

Ask the children to think of places in the world that need peace. There is a song that begins with the line, 'Let there be peace on earth and let it begin with me' (by Sy Miller and Jill Jackson). Ask the children also to think of situations in school where we need to help people to work together and where we can be peacemakers—for example, when children are squabbling over a ruler or a football. How can that situation be sorted out so that everyone can get along together?

You could remind the children that Jesus got on well with lots of different people—rich and poor, 'sinners' and 'religious people'. He even told us that we should love our enemies with the love that God gives us—quite a challenge! We're bound to like some people more than others, especially those who like the same games and activities as we do, but we are all part of a large team in school and need to work out a way to get along with everyone.

Suggestions for songs

- Peace, perfect peace (*Come and Praise* 53)
- Spirit of peace (*Come and Praise* 85)
- Peace is flowing (*Come and Praise* 144)
- Working together (*Every Colour under the Sun* 37)
- Together (*Songs for Every Assembly*—Out of the Ark)

Suggested prayer

Lord God, thank you for the message of the prophet Isaiah all those hundreds of years ago, which we still need to hear today. Help us to be peacemakers. Give us your help when we find it hard to love others. Let there be peace in your world and let it begin with me. Amen

Andrew the apostle

⟨ Assembly 1 ⟩

Passing on the message

The story about how Andrew became one of Jesus' first disciples, and his excitement in passing on the good news about Jesus, can act as a useful reflection on what we say about others. We can choose what information we pass on about other people and, indeed, how we spend our time thinking generally.

Bible links

One of the two men who had heard John and had gone with Jesus was Andrew, the brother of Simon Peter. The first thing Andrew did was to find his brother and tell him, 'We have found the Messiah!' The Hebrew word 'Messiah' means the same as the Greek word 'Christ.' Andrew brought his brother to Jesus. And when Jesus saw him, he said, 'Simon son of John, you will be called Cephas.' This name can be translated as 'Peter'.

JOHN 1:40–42

Key background information for the teacher

Andrew is the patron saint of Scotland, and Scots celebrate St Andrew's Day around the world on 30 November. The flag of

Scotland is the cross of St Andrew, and it is widely displayed as a symbol of national identity.

St Andrew is said to have been responsible for spreading the Christian message through Asia Minor and Greece. Tradition suggests that he was put to death by the Romans in southern Greece by being crucified on a diagonal cross. His bones were put in a tomb and, around 300 years later, were moved by Emperor Constantine the Great to his new capital Constantinople (now called Istanbul, in Turkey). Legend suggests that a Greek monk, or an Irish assistant of St Columba, called St Rule (or St Regulus), was warned in a dream that St Andrew's remains were to be moved, and was directed by an angel to take what he could of the remains to the 'ends of the earth' for safekeeping. St Rule dutifully followed these directions, removing a tooth, an arm bone, a kneecap and some fingers from St Andrew's tomb and transporting them as far away as he could. Scotland was close to the extremity of the known world at that time and it was here that St Rule was shipwrecked with his precious cargo.

Very little is really known about St Andrew himself. He is thought to have been a fisherman in Galilee, now part of Israel, along with his elder brother Simon Peter. The story of how both men became followers of Jesus is found in John 1:40–42.

Suggestions for visual aids and resources

- A speech bubble on an OHP or on a garden cane (see page 173 for speech bubble template)
- A grid on which to record children's ideas about positive and negative types of messages
- A telephone or note

Ideas for exploring the theme

Arrange for a note to be brought to you as the assembly opens. Alternatively, get a member of staff to phone you on your mobile during the assembly, or just pretend to receive a call on a telephone, or even a text message. This could be the basis for exploring with the children different ways of sending messages.

Make the link to the Bible by explaining how Jesus gathered a group of friends to help him with his work of getting his message of love across to people. Although his brother, Simon Peter, is perhaps more famous, it was Andrew who passed on the message that he had met someone special. Read the short section from John's Gospel (see 'Bible links' above). Andrew couldn't wait to pass on the news about Jesus to his brother. Ask what Andrew might have said. You could use a speech bubble to record the children's suggestions.

How important is it for us to pass on good news? Sometimes the news on television is full of the problems of the world, but the bulletins often end with something more positive, and this is also true of children's news bulletins.

How often do we open our ears to hear bad news about people or open our mouths to pass it on? It would make such a lot of difference if we decided not to pass on the bad news, but to make sure we talk about the positive things we hear or think. You could show some speech bubbles with wording to help children think positively, such as 'Thank you for…', 'I like the way you…', 'It's fun when…', and so on. Alternatively, make a list of positive and negative types of message—for example:

○ Positive: praise, thanks, compliments, invitations, birthday cards and so on.
○ Negative: telling tales, attracting attention to yourself, boasting and so on.

Ask the children to suggest other positive and negative types of messages. Encourage staff to continue this discussion in class as a PSHE topic.

Suggestions for songs

☉ God's people aren't super brave superheroes (*Kidsource* 86)
☉ He made me (*Come and Praise* 18)

Suggested prayer

Father God, help us to think well of other people and then to put these thoughts into action by thanking and praising others. Thank you for the special message from Jesus that God loves each one of us and wants us to know how special we are. Help us to treat others as special too. We know this will make you very happy. Amen

Andrew the apostle

Treasure in clay pots

This assembly explores the idea that God can use ordinary people who put themselves at his disposal. It links to the story of a varied but ordinary group of people, whom Jesus first invited to live and work alongside him. God still uses ordinary people today because he values each individual and sees his or her potential.

Bible links

We are not preaching about ourselves. Our message is that Jesus Christ is Lord... The Scriptures say, 'God commanded light to shine in the dark.' Now God is shining in our hearts to let you know that his glory is seen in Jesus Christ. We are like clay jars in which this treasure is stored. The real power comes from God and not from us.

2 CORINTHIANS 4:5–7

Key background information for the teacher

Paul uses the image of clay pots to make sure that the credit for what we achieve goes to God, who equips us with skills and talents as well as opportunities and challenges. Christians believe that God adds something extra—his life-changing power and love, his Holy Spirit in us—making our lives more purposeful. Knowing God is like a great treasure that we have been given. Those who acknowledge Jesus as Lord are called Christians and are open to be given God's Holy Spirit to be able to love and serve others.

Suggestions for visual aids and resources

- Two boxes—a jewellery box containing some ordinary bangles or a ribbon or hairband, and a plain box with a glamorous scarf or costume jewellery in it.
- Celebrity shots from a newspaper or magazine (optional)

Ideas for exploring the theme

Show the children the two boxes and ask them to predict what is inside each one. Get volunteers to open them. Were they surprised by what they discovered? Were they misled by the outward appearance of the box? You could show some pictures of celebrities from the supplements of a weekend newspaper. Often we admire these people. What sort of people are they? Are they attractive on the outside? What are they like on the inside? Point out that God looks at people in a way that ignores the outside (although he wants us to look after our bodies and keep fit and healthy) but is very interested in the sort of people we are on the inside.

Tell the following story, which reminds us of the same idea.

Tim tripped during the football match. The sole of one of his trainers came loose and started flapping. At half time he rushed to change them, knowing that the only other pair he had with him were his old ones, the ones he had worn on the way to the match. Later in the match, he had to take a penalty. 'Remember your training,' he told himself as he lined up on the spot, forgetting that he was no longer wearing his best trainers. He needed all his skills now. He focused and kicked the ball hard, right into the top corner of the net.

After the match, his friends joked with him about wearing his old trainers again for luck next time, but one of them pointed out that Tim could have scored in his wellies. 'It's the skill that counts—though I'm sure he'll be nagging his mum for some new trainers tonight!' said the friend.

Ask the children what they think the story tells us. Tease out the idea that Tim had the fooballing skills and it helped to have a good pair of trainers, but that his confidence came from his preparation and training, not from what he was wearing or what his trainers looked like on the outside. In the same way, God is interested in what sort of people we decide to be and our attitude towards him and others.

In his letter to the Christians in Galatia, Paul describes the fruit that will grow in our lives if they are lived for God. He says, 'God's Spirit makes us loving, happy, peaceful, patient, kind, good, faithful, gentle, and self-controlled. There is no law against behaving in any of these ways' (Galatians 5:22–23).

This theme could be explored further with *older* children in class by using a film clip from near the end of *Indiana Jones and the Last Crusade*. The scene is the one where the knight asks the first seeker for the grail to choose which of the cups on display is the one used by Jesus at the Last Supper. The mind of the seeker is confused by his greed and his assumption that the grail will be a rich-looking container. Indiana makes the right choice because he knows that Jesus came from a humble carpenter's family (I expect he listened well in his RE lessons at school!). Indiana is also guided by his desire to heal his dying father with water from the cup. Of course, in the film, the grail turns out to be a plain container—but its use has given it extraordinary power. (**NB:** Bear in mind that the film has a PG certificate, and this scene is particularly likely to frighten younger children because of the result of the first seeker's wrong choice!)

Suggestions for songs

⚙ He made me (*Come and Praise* 18)
⚙ Jesus' love is very wonderful (*Kidsource* 208)

Suggested prayer

Thank you, Lord God, that you don't judge by what you see on the outside. Thank you that each one of us is special to you. Help us to become better on the inside by following the example of Jesus. Amen

✠

Nicholas, Bishop of Myra

Three bags of gold

This assembly features the main story told about Saint Nicholas. Its focus is on his generosity and how he quietly went about showing God's love in his actions, but without drawing attention to himself. In this way it also reflects an attitude that Jesus valued, shown when he complimented the woman who gave her small but significant offering to the temple funds, compared to the man who made a big show of his generosity.

Bible links

When you do good deeds, don't try to show off. If you do, you won't get a reward from your Father in heaven. When you give to the poor, don't blow a loud horn. That's what show-offs do in the meeting places and on the street corners, because they are always looking for praise. I can assure you that they already have their reward. When you give to the poor, don't let anyone know about it. Then your gift will be given in secret. Your Father knows what is done in secret, and he will reward you.

MATTHEW 6:1–4

Jesus was sitting in the temple near the offering box and watching people put in their gifts. He noticed that many rich people were giving a lot of money. Finally, a poor widow came up and put in two coins that were worth only a few pennies. Jesus told his disciples to gather around him. Then he said: I tell you that this poor widow has put in more than all the others. Everyone else gave what they didn't need. But she is very poor and gave everything she had. Now she doesn't have a penny to live on.

MARK 12:41–44

Key background information for the teacher

Make whatever links are necessary back to the assembly about saints that you might have used at the beginning of November, or to St Andrew, which you might have marked on 30 November.

The special day to remember St Nicholas is celebrated on 6 December. St Nicholas is certainly an interesting character. It's rather difficult to separate legend from reality in the many stories related about him. You will also need to be careful, especially with younger children in the assembly, not to major on the fact that many adults believe he is the forerunner to our modern image of Santa Claus or Father Christmas, as you may risk shattering the mystery of who delivers those presents before Christmas morning!

Suggestions for visual aids and resources

○ Three bags of chocolate money
○ Children to act out the story as it is told (optional)

Ideas for exploring the theme

Explain that the assembly is about St Nicholas. You might choose to make a link back to other recent assemblies on saints if you have used them. It might also be useful to refer to the introduction on saints on page 55. In many countries, gifts are given on 6 December to remember St Nicholas' kindness, although in other places the gift-giving centres around Epiphany on 6 January. In the UK, gift giving centres around Christmas Day.

Nicholas was the Bishop of Myra in Asia (in modern Turkey) in the fourth century. Far from being a stuffy, distant sort of person, as some bishops might have been at that time, he was very concerned about people's family difficulties. However, being a rather shy man, he didn't like to do anything publicly to draw attention to himself. On one occasion, there was a man who had three daughters but could not pay the dowry (special marriage money paid to the groom's family) for his first daughter's marriage. Nicholas crept to the man's house and tossed a bag of coins in through the window. (In some versions of the story, he tosses the coins down the chimney, where they land in the stockings hung up to dry on the mantelpiece. If this was the case, he was either a very good shot or a good climber!)

The third time he did this—having treated each of the three daughters to his help—Nicholas was spotted by the father, and news about his generosity spread. You may wish to point out here that St Nicholas' story draws a parallel with Jesus, who asked the people he healed not to spread the news that he had made them well.

The story could be told as a dramatic presentation, prepared with some children in advance. Chocolate money could be used as a visual aid during the storytelling, and as a reward for the volunteers. Link the story to the Bible passages above, reminding the children how Jesus liked people to give without being too showy or wanting attention, just as Nicholas did, to please God.

Suggestions for songs

- ✿ Shake a friend's hand (*Kidsource* 293)
- ✿ Seek ye first the kingdom of God (*Kidsource* 292)
- ✿ Jesus' hands were kind hands (*Kidsource* 194)

Suggested prayer

Thank you, Lord, for the example of St Nicholas, who has become famous for his kindness in helping a family in need. Help us to be both like him and like Jesus in helping others. Thank you for the tradition we have of giving presents to show our love and care. Help us to choose well and enjoy giving cards and presents to one another when Christmas comes. Amen

Nicholas, Bishop of Myra

Assembly 2

God loves a generous giver

St Nicholas was a super example of someone who spotted a need and responded with compassion and practical help. Challenge the children to invent a story or to find examples of others who have done the same. This could be tackled as a drama for an assembly. The story below makes a similar point, treating Tim's response as something that is recognized by others and brings its own reward.

Bible links

The group of believers all felt the same way about everything. None of them claimed that their possessions were their own, and they shared everything they had with each other.
ACTS 4:32

Each of you must make up your own mind about how much to give. But don't feel sorry that you must give and don't feel that you are forced to give. God loves people who love to give. God can bless you with everything you need, and you will always have more than enough to do all kinds of good things for others.
2 CORINTHIANS 9:7–8

Key background information for the teacher

There are many examples in Paul's letters where he praises the generosity of the believers in one church who are supporting another church financially—and, indeed, supporting his ministry, although he also points out that he works as a tent maker to avoid being a burden to anyone. He emphasizes that our giving to the work of the church should be from our hearts rather than out of a sense of duty—a response to the love shown to us by God and the changing priorities in our lives. Early Christians are recorded in Acts as sharing their possessions, so that no one was in need.

It may be that your school supports a particular charity in the run-up to Christmas, such as the Blue Peter appeal or the Samaritans' Purse Shoebox appeal, which you could feature in this assembly as a part of the story.

Suggestions for visual aids and resources

⊛ Notepad and pencil

Ideas for exploring the theme

Ask the children if they have ever saved up money for something, either for themselves or as a present for someone else. Take two or three examples, or let the children have one minute to tell their neighbour about it before stopping at an agreed signal, such as a hand raised in the air.

Now pretend you are making a list of things you need to buy, and include a present for someone. It could be that you are getting organized for Christmas. Talk to yourself about it: 'I can't wait to see Mum's face when she opens it. I know it's just what she wants. Anyway, I was going to tell you a story about Tim today: his present buying didn't quite go as planned.'

Tell the following story:

Tim was saving up to buy a CD for his mum. He was also saving up to buy a new pair of trainers, which were in the sale at the sports shop. He'd been saving his pocket money and earning extra by doing jobs for friends and neighbours, such as car washing. The problem was, he'd also seen an advert on television by a children's charity, and he couldn't get it out of his mind. He really wanted to help, and it seemed right, as Christmas got nearer, to help others. He left it a couple more days, but the feeling was still there, so he decided to send £5.

It was time to go shopping, and Tim put his wallet in his pocket and set off with his mum. At the shopping centre, he and Mum went off to different shops and he bought the CD she liked, making sure he hid it deep in his pocket so that she wouldn't see it. He then went to the sports shop where he'd seen the trainers. 'Oh no!' he said out loud—the 'Sale' signs had gone from the window and the price had gone back up. It was almost time to meet up with Mum again.

Mum noticed that Tim had no bag with him and asked what had happened. At first, he didn't want to talk about it, but she asked him whether he'd lost some of his money. He explained that the sale had finished and how he'd given some of his money to the children's charity. Now he no longer had enough.

'Come on,' said Mum, 'let's look in a couple of other shops to compare prices.' They couldn't find any other trainers as good as the ones he wanted, so Mum took Tim back to the first shop to check the price. 'How much have you got?' she asked him.

'I'm £4 short of what I need,' he replied.

'OK,' said Mum, 'I'll give you the rest of the money. You

weren't to know the sale would end, and I do feel proud of you for supporting the charity. It was a kind thing to do.'

Tim was so pleased and beamed a big smile at his mum.

Read the Bible passage from 2 Corinthians 9 (see 'Bible links' above), pointing out that giving to others and a generous attitude are things that please God.

Christians believe that God was very generous in sending Jesus to be born as a baby at Christmas so that he could show God's love to everyone in a new way. Christians want to respond to God's love by showing love, care and generosity to others.

Suggestions for songs

- ☉ Give me oil in my lamp (*Come and Praise* 43)
- ☉ When I needed a neighbour (*Come and Praise* 65)
- ☉ When I survey the wondrous cross (If the children do not know this hymn, the words of the last verse could be read as the children listen and reflect on them.) (*Hymns Old and New* 549; *The Source* 572)
- ☉ When I think about the cross (*Kidsource* 376; *Songs for Every Easter*—Out of the Ark)

Suggested prayer

Say the Lord's Prayer together and finish with the prayer below.

Thank you, Lord God, for the chances we have to put a smile on people's faces with a card and a present. Thank you for the charities who work so hard to make people's lives better. Thank you for the times when we are able to help them in their work. (Mention a particular charity here if it is appropriate to your school situation.) *Amen*

Advent

Traditionally, Advent is the period of the Christian calendar leading up to Christmas. It is a time of preparation and increasing readiness to celebrate the festival (especially on each of the four Sundays leading up to Christmas Day). In the past, it would have been a time when people may have fasted or gone without, in order to have more to celebrate at Christmas both in real and spiritual terms.

The word Advent means 'coming' or 'arrival'. It is a time not only of looking forward, but also of reflecting on the past. This can be done by remembering old friends not seen very often (perhaps, nowadays, by sending greetings cards) or reflecting on words in the Bible that tell us to prepare our hearts, some of which remind us that Jesus promised to return one final time at a date unannounced, and challenged us to be ready. For Christians, it is also a time for reflecting on the biblical story of salvation and God's involvement with humankind.

Because the school term often finishes before the end of Advent and Christmas needs to be celebrated early, the themes of Advent can be followed using an Advent crown. The crown has five candles, each representing a different part of the Advent story. The candles can be lit with appropriate spacing to allow all five to be explored before the end of term, with the final one symbolizing Jesus, the light for the world. You may wish to invite parents and carers to one of the Advent assemblies.

Traditional themes include:

- ✪ The patriarchs
- ✪ The prophets
- ✪ John the Baptist
- ✪ Mary, the mother of Jesus
- ✪ Jesus

Advent

Assembly 1

The patriarchs

Matthew wrote his Gospel for a Jewish readership and was keen to show that Jesus fitted firmly into the Jews' historic perspective. Matthew sets out to show us that the history of God's involvement in the world goes right back to those who were the founding fathers of the nation of Israel—Abraham, Isaac and Jacob—all of whom had a special contract, or covenant, with God.

Bible links

Jesus Christ came from the family of King David and also from the family of Abraham… There were fourteen generations from Abraham to David. There were also fourteen generations from David to the exile in Babylonia and fourteen more to the birth of the Messiah.
MATTHEW 1:1 and 17

Key background information for the teacher

This assembly links Jesus back to his ancestors, setting him firmly in the Jewish tradition and presenting him as an integral part of the ongoing history of God and his chosen people. Christians believe that Jesus is the pinnacle of God's rescue plan for the whole world.

Suggestions for visual aids and resources

⊛ The family tree of a famous person such as Queen Elizabeth II (see www.smartdraw.com for a photo version, or, for a traditional tree, www.royal.gov.uk). Alternatively, interview a member of staff about their own family tree.

⊛ Matthew 1:1–17 (the list of Jesus' ancestors) on an OHT (see Worksheet 4, which can be downloaded free of charge from the 'Books and resources' section of the Barnabas website, www.barnabasinschools.org.uk).

⊛ An Advent crown, with four purple candles around the outside and one larger white candle in the centre

Ideas for exploring the theme

Show the family tree of a famous person or have someone primed to reveal information about their own family (check that they know back to their grandparents and interview them about the members of their family, possibly making a visual family tree for all to see). Do they know any further back? Explain that many grown-ups are fascinated to find out about their ancestors and to discover whether there is anyone famous in their family line.

Explain how, at the beginning of Matthew's Gospel (written for a Jewish readership), Matthew gives a detailed list of the generations of famous ancestors of Jesus. Matthew shows us how Jesus is linked to David, and David is linked right back to the founders of the Jewish faith—Abraham, Isaac and Jacob, who are known as the patriarchs.

Light the first Advent candle, which is the candle for the patriarchs.

You might like to show the list of Jesus' ancestors on an OHT and ask the children if they spot any names they recognize. They could raise a hand every time they hear a name they know while you read out (some of) the list.

One of the points Matthew was making was how God has cared for generation after generation of Jesus' family. Each new generation had its ups and downs, but each one was challenged to make a commitment to follow God's ways in their time and place. The family tree also explains why Joseph had to take his wife, Mary (pregnant with the baby Jesus), back to his home town of Bethlehem for the census. Through this, a prediction by the prophet Micah, that the Messiah would be born in the small town of Bethlehem, came true. It's amazing to think that God was not just looking after his own people, but was also even turning events such as the Roman census to his own uses.

Still today, Christians believe that God cares for all those who trust him with their family's future. He wants everyone to follow his teaching, which we can read about in the Bible, especially in the life and words of his Son, Jesus. God has looked after those who have followed his ways for many generations and still does so today. He is always ready to listen to us, just as he listened to people who followed his ways in Bible times.

Suggestions for songs

- While shepherds watched their flocks by night (*Hymns Old and New* 554; *Sing Nowell*)
- O little town of Bethlehem (*Hymns Old and New* 377; *The Source* 393; *Sing Nowell*)

Suggested prayer

Thank you for our families and those who care for us. Thank you for the reminder today that you care for your family and friends for years and years in each new generation. Thank you for the believers who have passed on the message about you from Abraham to today, and for Christian leaders who try to explain to us why Jesus is still so important. Amen

Advent

The prophets

This assembly explores the role played by the Old Testament prophets who predicted the coming of a Messiah. Advent is a time when people look forward not just to celebrating the birth of Jesus, but also to welcoming him when he comes again.

Bible links

A virgin is pregnant; she will have a son and will name him Immanuel.

ISAIAH 7:14b

Those who walked in the dark have seen a bright light... A child has been born for us... [the] Prince of Peace... He will rule David's kingdom and make it grow strong.

ISAIAH 9:2 and 6–7 (ABRIDGED)

Like a branch that sprouts from a stump, someone from David's family will some day be king. The Spirit of the Lord will be with him to give him understanding, wisdom, and insight.

ISAIAH 11:1–2a

Someone is shouting: 'Clear a path in the desert! Make a straight road for the Lord our God.'
ISAIAH 40:3

Bethlehem… you are one of the smallest towns in the nation of Judah. But the Lord will choose one of your people to rule the nation—someone whose family goes back to ancient times.
MICAH 5:2

Key background information for the teacher

It was important to the Gospel writers to be able to show that Jesus' arrival had been predicted hundreds of years before. The prophets of the Old Testament had more than one role. First of all, they summoned people back to the revealed way of God. Second, they predicted future key events, although it was often unclear when these predictions would come true. The Bible is testimony to events that have come true, such as the birth of Christ, and records events still to come, such as his second coming.

Suggestions for visual aids and resources

◎ An OHT of the words from the Jewish prophets as listed in the 'Bible links'
◎ Four giant jigsaw shapes that fit together so that they can be turned over to reveal the words GOD IS WITH US. (One word needs to be on each piece so that the jigsaw is meaningless until joined together)
◎ An Advent crown, with four purple candles around the outside and one larger white candle in the centre

Ideas for exploring the theme

Explain that today we are looking at the way Jesus' birth was predicted by God's prophets many years before Jesus was born. People passed down the promises about God's anointed king, or Messiah, from generation to generation, believing that one day the promise would come true. Just before Jesus was born, the Romans took over the nation of Israel and the Jewish people felt that their freedom was limited. This would have heightened their expectation that God would send his promised king to rescue them from Roman rule.

Introduce each of the promises from the 'Bible links'. Explain to the children that the job of a prophet was both to predict what would happen in the future and to remind people of how they should behave in the present. Explain, as you turn over the pieces of the jigsaw, that the promises all pointed forward to the time when God would come among his people. The word Immanuel (or Emmanuel) means 'God is with us'.

Light the second Advent candle, which is the candle for the prophets.

Many of the Old Testament prophecies were used in a famous piece of music called *Messiah* by George Frederick Handel, some of which is often performed in Christmas concerts. You might like to play part of it to the children or say that you will leave it playing as they leave the room.

God made promises long ago that he would send a special messenger, his own Son, Jesus. The Bible is full of promises that God made and kept. Some of them are promises that are for us today. Here are some examples.

I tell you for certain that if you have faith in me, you will do the same things that I am doing. You will do even greater things, now that I am going back to the Father.
JOHN 14:12

But the Holy Spirit will come and help you, because the Father will send the Spirit to take my place. The Spirit will teach you everything and will remind you of what I said while I was with you.

JOHN 14:26

I will be with you always, even until the end of the world.

MATTHEW 28:20

Are we good at making promises? Ask the children if they can think of a promise that they made and have kept, or perhaps one that they had difficulty keeping. (Pause for thought.)

Explain that God is faithful and loyal. We can rely on him, so we should try be the sort of people who can be relied on—people who keep their promises.

Suggestions for songs

❂ Once in royal David's city (Hymns Old and New 404)
❂ Light a candle (Come and Praise 118)
❂ Like a candle flame (The Source 322)

Suggestions for music

❂ Handel's Messiah Part 1: numbers 3, 8–9, 11–12

Suggested prayer

Loving God, thank you that you sent your prophets as messengers long ago and that they predicted the birth of your Son, Jesus. Thank you for Jesus' birth. Thank you that he brought hope into people's lives, like a light appearing in the darkness. Help us to learn by listening to his words. Amen

Advent

John the Baptist

This assembly explores the idea of preparing for someone special, and how, at this time of the year, we spend a lot of time on Christmas preparations but easily lose sight of the reason for the celebration in the flurry of activity. John challenges us about getting our priorities right and helps us to remember to listen to God's message and then act on it.

Bible links

This is the good news about Jesus Christ, the Son of God. It began just as God had said in the book written by Isaiah the prophet, 'I am sending my messenger to get the way ready for you. In the desert someone is shouting, "Get the road ready for the Lord! Make a straight path for him."' So John the Baptist appeared in the desert and told everyone, 'Turn back to God and be baptized! Then your sins will be forgiven.'

MARK 1:1–4

Key background information for the teacher

The prophet Isaiah explained that someone would come to prepare the way for God's special rescuer, his Messiah. This messenger would act as a warm-up before Jesus took centre stage and, although he would attract a lot of attention, he was meant to point the way towards the Messiah and raise people's expectations. In his own right John was destined, like the prophets before him, to draw back to God people whose lives had taken a wrong turning. The sign that they were sorry and wanted to make a fresh start in life was being baptized, a practice that has continued in the Christian Church ever since.

Suggestions for visual aids and resources

- ☼ Copies of the script below
- ☼ If time allows for you to extend the assembly a little, you could use templates for different road signs: rectangle, triangle and circle
- ☼ An Advent crown, with four purple candles around the outside and one larger white candle in the centre

Ideas for exploring the theme

Use the prepared script of an 'interview' with John the Baptist (see pp. 116–117). It may be best if you take the role of John and explain to the children that you have arranged to be interviewed. Explain that John was Jesus' cousin and lived in the desert. He ate simple food and wore rough clothes.

If possible, practise the script beforehand with an older child or another member of staff. This will make it run more smoothly, but is not essential. The more 'improvised' John's replies, the slicker it will seem. The interviewer can have the questions on a clipboard.

Interviewer: I am standing here at the edge of the desert in Judea, where crowds of people have been coming out to be baptized in the River Jordan by a wild-looking man who has been living rough in the desert. I am hoping we might get to speak to this man, who has been calling on people to turn away from the things they have done wrong and be washed clean, making a new start in life... And here he is. Hello, there, can you please tell us who you are and a bit about yourself.

John: My name is John and I'm the son of Elizabeth and Zechariah. My dad is one of the temple priests.

Interviewer: Well, John, you seem to have made quite a name for yourself out here in the desert. What do you survive on out here?

John: I usually collect berries and search for honey. Quite often recently, I've been able to catch locusts. Quite a decent diet—though not a lot of variety and the locust legs do get stuck between your teeth!

Interviewer: If you don't mind me saying, you seem to have let yourself go a bit, with your long hair and unusual clothes.

John: Well, it's not really been top of my list to get to the hairdressers, and what would I need the latest fashions for? It's much more important to spend my time reminding everyone about what sort of people God wants us to be.

Interviewer: We hear you've been drawing a lot of attention to yourself, making a good deal of noise. What exactly is your message?

John: I expect you know the words of the prophet Isaiah, 'Get the road ready for the Lord!' Well, he's coming! It's not really about me getting lots of attention. You see, I'm just here to announce his coming. It's time to put your life in order, to get ready, to tune in to what God is saying—you need to get ready to listen to what he has to say. When you meet him, you'll realize that I'm not even worthy to untie his sandals.

Interviewer: That's quite a message!

John: Let's talk some more. You're welcome to come and have dinner with me, if you want to. I'm afraid it's locust and leaf stir-fry again... (*Walks off, pretending to talk some more*)

Explain that, through John, God was getting things ready for the arrival of Jesus. Advent is a special time when we prepare to celebrate Jesus' birth, but Advent also reminds us about how Jesus grew up to teach people about God. Today it is still good to be reminded that Advent and Christmas are not just about sending cards and presents, but they are times to think about listening to what God is saying to us.

Light the third Advent candle, which is the candle for John the Baptist.

If you have time to extend the assembly, you could discuss the shapes of different road signs. Tease out the fact that each shape is linked to a different type of sign: circles for orders, triangles for

Reproduced with permission from *Assemblies for Autumn Festivals* published by BRF 2007 (1 84101 459 1)

www.barnabasinschools.org.uk

warnings and rectangles for information. What might John put into these different shapes? What might he give as his most important piece of information? *(Jesus is coming!)* What warning might he give? *(You need to make a U-turn!)* What order might he give? *(Listen to what God is saying!)*.

Suggestions for songs

- ❂ Joy to the world (or a carol of your choosing) *(Hymns Old and New* 283; *The Source* 305)
- ❂ On Jordan's bank (you could use words from it to introduce the prayer) *(Hymns Old and New* 401)

Suggested prayer

On Jordan's bank the Baptist cry
Announces that the Lord is nigh.
Awake and hearken, for he brings
Glad tidings of the king of kings.
CHARLES COFFIN (1676–1749)

We pray for all those who claim to be followers of Jesus today. Help them to worship you and to care for the people they meet. Help us to listen well to the words of Jesus in the Bible. We ask you to show us anything that is not right in our lives and help us to become better people. Amen

Advent

Mary, the mother of Jesus

This assembly focuses on one of the most famous women in history, Mary the mother of Jesus. She is an essential part of the Advent and Christmas narrative. A key lesson we can learn from her is her willingness to obey God, despite the fact that it would throw her world upside down. Following God's path for our lives will rarely be as alarming as Mary's experience was, but, for those who want to follow closely where he leads, life will undoubtedly have its challenges. Mary must have awaited the birth of her son with a mixture of excitement and nervousness.

Bible links

God sent the angel Gabriel to the town of Nazareth in Galilee with a message for a virgin named Mary. She was engaged to Joseph from the family of King David.

LUKE 1:26–27

A short time later Mary hurried to a town in the hill country of Judea. She went into Zechariah's home, where she greeted Elizabeth.

LUKE 1:39–40

Key background information for the teacher

As a teenage mother-to-be, Mary faced potential disaster: she might have been cast out by her family and friends. She must have been truly relieved when Joseph, her fiancé, agreed to stand by her and marry her. However, it is easy to understand her decision to go and stay with relatives—in fact, with Elizabeth, who was soon to give birth to John the Baptist. As they met, Elizabeth's baby moved within her and both women were given a special prophetic message from God. Mary's humility and obedience remind us how God uses ordinary people to fulfil his extraordinary purposes.

Suggestions for visual aids and resources

❂ Pictures of the annunciation and Mary's visit to Elizabeth (see www.nationalgallery.org.uk. Click on 'Collections' and then enter keywords in 'Search')
❂ The names of two famous people written on folded pieces of paper, ready for the question and answer games
❂ An Advent crown, with four purple candles around the outside and one larger white candle in the centre

Ideas for exploring the theme

Play a 'guess who' game at the start by pretending to be a famous person. Children ask questions about your identity, to which you answer 'yes' or 'no'. Alternatively, play the 'yes/no' game, in which the words 'yes' and 'no' are banned and you try to catch someone out by asking them questions. See who can last the longest before saying 'yes' or 'no'.

Explain that today's assembly is about someone who had to decide 'yes' or 'no' when she was brought an important message. She was neither important nor famous but had been chosen by God to give birth to his baby son. Make the link that Mary was engaged to Joseph, whose ancestry could be traced back 28 generations to Abraham (see Worksheet Two).

Ask the children what scene they most associate with Mary. Suggestions might include the visit from the angel Gabriel, the visit to her relative Elizabeth, the journey to Bethlehem, the arrival in Bethlehem to find no room at the inn, the birth of Jesus, the arrival of shepherds (and later the wise men), or fleeing the anger and jealousy of King Herod. The different scenes could be allocated to different classes to produce a whole-school display.

Show the children a painting of the annunciation (which means 'announcement') to help them imagine the thoughts running through Gabriel's and Mary's minds before, during and after this event. Imagine how differently things would have turned out if Mary had not said 'yes'.

Light the fourth Advent candle, which is the candle for Mary.

The story continues with Mary's visit to her cousin Elizabeth, who was also expecting a baby. When Mary arrived, Elizabeth felt her own baby move in her womb. Her greeting is very famous: 'God has blessed you more than any other woman! He has also blessed the child you will have. Why should the mother of my Lord come to me?' (Luke 1:42–43)

It must have been a relief to Mary that Elizabeth recognized how special the baby was. Mary burst into a song of praise. Her song, which is also very famous, is known as the Magnificat, a Latin word meaning 'make great'. The song reminds us how God uses humble people and has been faithful to his people since the time of Abraham:

With all my heart I praise the Lord, and I am glad because of God my Saviour. He cares for me, his humble servant. From now on, all people will say God has blessed me. God All-Powerful has done great things for me, and his name is holy.

LUKE 1:46–49

Suggestions for songs

- ❁ The angel Gabriel from heaven came (*Hymns Old and New* 471; *Merrily to Bethlehem* 2)
- ❁ Spirit of the living God (*The Source* 462 and 463; *Hymns Old and New* 454 and 455)
- ❁ Praise my soul, the king of heaven (*The Source* 433; *Hymns Old and New* 422)

Suggested prayer

Thank you, Lord God, that Mary said 'yes' and trusted your plan for her life. Thank you for her excitement as she looked forward to the future, even though it must have been more than a bit scary. Help us to enjoy the excitement of this time of the year and remember how important the coming of Jesus is. Amen

Advent

Assembly 5

Jesus pitches his tent

This assembly reminds us of the joint human and divine nature of Jesus. He is truly God in that he is the Son of God, but also truly human in that he was born of a human mother. It's quite an amazing thought, that God became flesh so that we could get to know him better. As John puts it, 'The Word became a human being and lived here with us' (John 1:14). A literal translation would be '... pitched his tent among us'. God's clear intention was to 'get stuck in', to get involved more fully in the world he had brought into being. The implication is that his followers are also expected to get involved in helping others and showing God's love in action.

Bible links

In the beginning was the one who is called the Word. The Word was with God and was truly God. From the very beginning the Word was with God. And with this Word, God created all things. Nothing was made without the Word. Everything that was created received its life from him, and his life gave light to everyone... God sent a man called John, who came to tell about the light and to lead all people to have faith. John wasn't that light. He came only to tell about the light... The Word became a human being and lived here with us. We saw his true glory, the glory of the only Son of the Father. From him all the kindness and all the truth of God have come down to us.

JOHN 1:1–4, 6–8 and 14

Key background information for the teacher

This Bible passage is traditionally used at Christmas carol services and would keep a preacher busy for many minutes with its rich seam of ideas. It ties together the concepts explored over Advent— that the coming of Jesus was part of a long-intended rescue plan by God for the salvation of people; that his special message, or 'Word', was in fact his Son; that although Jesus was born of a human mother, he was divine; and that John was the herald of Jesus' coming.

Jesus lived in the world for a few brief years, rather like someone travelling through—hence the image of someone pitching a tent. This reminds us of Jesus travelling around the country from place to place, teaching and healing. It also links to the story of God's people escaping from Egypt and travelling towards their promised land, setting up camp and waiting for God to show the next step, though beset by many acts of disobedience towards God and resisting Moses' leadership.

Suggestions for visual aids and resources

☼ A small tent or a drawing of a tent (a triangular prism shape is fine)
☼ The Bible passage from John 1 on OHT (optional)
☼ An Advent crown, with four purple candles around the outside and one larger white candle in the centre

Ideas for exploring the theme

Ask who goes camping with their family. Ask for suggestions about what is needed on a camping trip. Focus on the tent and draw out the idea that you can move a tent from place to place, seeing different places and meeting many different people.

Now refer to the Hebrew people, God's chosen nation, travelling towards the promised land and living in tents for over 40 years. (Nowadays, travelling people are known as nomads.) They had one special tent, called the tabernacle, where God was worshipped. This was carried from place to place as the people travelled through the desert.

Move on to ask if the children know how long Jesus lived on earth and if they can give examples of some of the places he lived in or visited—for example, Bethlehem, Nazareth, Cana, Capernaum and Jerusalem. Explain that it is thought that, up to the age of 30, Jesus lived and worked as a carpenter in Nazareth. This information is based on the fact that his (earthly) father Joseph was a carpenter, and that the family home was in Nazareth. After this, Jesus travelled around the country, telling people about God. You could ask the children for examples of things he did, for a quick thumbnail sketch—for example, teaching, healing, performing miracles, telling people stories about God and so on. Read the passage from John's Gospel, explaining that the words in verse 14 originally meant 'pitched his tent among us'.

Light the fifth Advent candle, which is the candle for Jesus, the light for the world.

Anyone who has been camping will know that part of the attraction is the freedom to move from place to place, but also that it is so easy to strike up conversations with fellow campers. Jesus was someone who got involved with people, showing God's love in action. Those people who say they are his friends today are called to be like him.

Suggestions for songs

- When I needed a neighbour (*Come and Praise* 65)
- Jesus' love is very wonderful (*Kidsource* 208)
- He came down that we might have love (*World Praise* 27: number varies according to edition)

Suggested prayer

Lord Jesus, thank you that you do not hold us at arm's length. Help us to be more like you, showing your kind of love to others so that the world may become a better place. Amen

PART TWO

Ideas for
cross-curricular work

Harvest

Curriculum link: RE

As well as looking at how people of different faiths and cultures celebrate harvest, RE also links to the key themes of bread and water. These can be explored through the symbolism of Jesus as both the bread of life and living water, the water of baptism, or the use of bread and wine in Holy Communion. You could contact a local minister to explain how these symbols are used in worship.

Bible links

Psalms 8 and 65 are often used at harvest time, as well as Psalm 148 and Psalm 136 (omitting verses 10–22), which has a response already written into it 'God's love never fails'. Others to consider are Psalm 19:1–6, Psalm 95:1–7 and Psalm 93:1–4 (verse 1 works well as a refrain between each of the other verses). The Dramatized Bible shows some very useful ways of performing psalms, or you could make up your own, such as the example below, which reflects the different themes typically found in the psalms.

Leader 1:   O Lord, we praise you for all you have done in our world.
Leader 2:   You care for the fields filled with grain.
Group 2:   You feed the crops with your nutritious rain.
Leader 1:   The hillsides shall dance and clap their hands,
Group 1:   So tall, looking over your beautiful lands.
Leader 2:   The streams jump and dance away,
Group 2:   Reflecting the blue sky upon this beautiful day.

Leader 1: The sheep roam the meadows, basking in the sun,

Group 1: And thanks to your land, Lord, we can all have fun.

Leader 2: The trees bear fruit for us all to eat.

Group 2: You help us through the hard times we are likely to meet.

All: Glory to the Father, and to the Son, and to the Holy Spirit; as it was in the beginning, is now, and shall be for ever. Amen

Other appropriate Bible passages include:

- ❂ Matthew 13:1–9 (The parable of the farmer)
- ❂ Matthew 4:18–22 (Jesus chooses four fishermen)
- ❂ Matthew 9:35–37 (Jesus has pity on people)
- ❂ Genesis 1—2:4a (the story of creation)
- ❂ Matthew 6:25–30 (God's care for us and all his creatures)
- ❂ Matthew 10:29–31 (God counts every hair on our head)
- ❂ Luke 9:10–17 (Jesus feeds five thousand)
- ❂ 1 Kings 17:1–7 (Elijah is fed by the ravens)
- ❂ 1 Kings 17:8–16 (Elijah helps a widow in Zarephath)
- ❂ Ruth 1—4 (a story of friendship, loyalty and romance in the context of a harvest story—great for drama!)

Ideas for exploring the theme

1. Write the words HARVEST FESTIVAL on the board and ask the children how many shorter words they can make with the letters. Now pick out the words that link with the harvest theme. Ask the children to suggest how these words might be joined together to explain the theme. For example, you can make the words SHARE, FAIR, STARVE, FEAR, FEAST, FRESH.

Alternatively, arrange for children to hold up the original letters and then move forward into position for each new word. A narrator could then explain each word. If the cards are numbered and a pattern typed up on the back of each card, it may make it easier for children to practise getting into position quickly. For example, number the words from 1 to 15. The pattern for the word 'share' would then be 6, 1, 2, 3, 5. A drum roll on a tambour or side drum can be used to add excitement and indicate a change of word.

2. Write the word HARVEST down the left-hand side of a piece of paper. Ask the children for ideas to do with harvest that begin with each letter. This could become an acrostic-style list poem or could be used as a prayer if read out and finished with a sentence such as, 'Thank you, Father God, for all these things. Amen.'

Alternatively, make a mesostic poem by writing the letters of the keyword down the centre of the paper and choosing related words that have the letters of the keyword in them, but not necessarily at the beginning of the word. A mesostic poem can end up looking rather like the branches of a tree, with the keyword forming the central trunk.

Suggestions for songs
- All things bright and beautiful (*Come and Praise* 3)
- Think of a world without any flowers (*Come and Praise* 17)
- Pears and apples (*Come and Praise* 135)
- Lord of the harvest (*Come and Praise* 133)
- He's got the whole world in his hands (*Come and Praise* 19)
- Have you heard the raindrops? (*Come and Praise* 2)
- I listen (*Come and Praise* 60)
- Autumn days (*Come and Praise* 4)
- Thank you, Lord, for this fine day (*Come and Praise* 32)
- All the nations of the earth (*Come and Praise* 14)
- Who put the colours in the rainbow? (*Come and Praise* 12)
- When I needed a neighbour (*Come and Praise* 65)
- Who's the king of the jungle? (*Kidsource* 388)
- My God is so big (*Kidsource* 255; also in *Junior Praise*)

Songs for Every Season from Out of the Ark Music is another very useful resource, with a CD providing a choir and instrumental backing for each song. Examples from this book include 'Harvest Song (There is a farmer)' and 'Turn back the clocks'.

Traditional hymns include:

☻ Come ye (or you) thankful people come (*Hymns Old and New* 101)
☻ We plough the fields and scatter (*Hymns Old and New* 534)

Younger children often enjoy taking a familiar song and adapting it with new words. For example, 'Thank you, Lord, for this fine day' works well if you replace the words 'this fine day' with other ideas. You could also use nursery rhymes such as 'Old MacDonald had a farm' with harvest ideas added, such as 'And on that farm he grew some wheat', or with animal verses to give you a chance to make the customary noises!

Suggested prayers

1. Give the children a structure to complete such as:

Thank you for the world you made.
Thank you for…
You made…
You designed…
Help us to care for this beautiful world. Amen

2. Use a responsive prayer:

Leader: Creator God, you have made a wonderful world.
Response: Help us to look after it well.
Leader: You created/made… (add ideas of your own to evoke the response)
Response: Help us to look after it/them well.

3. Lord, give us eyes to appreciate just how amazing this world is. We worship and thank you for:

The ever-changing clouds…
The majesty of the night sky…
The joy of making friends…
The beauty of a sunset…

Add to the above list, then finish with a phrase such as, 'Creator God, we give you thanks. Amen.'

4. Create a prayer that shows understanding of who we rely on in a long chain from farmer to shop assistant for providing our food. It is important to recognize that harvest time often reflects an emphasis on the time when Britain was largely changing from a farming community to an industrial one. It is useful not just to think of the created world, but also of manufactured goods, thanking God for those who supply our fuel and for inventions that make our lives easier.

5. Think of the ways in which the world's resources are shared unfairly or wasted and turn your thoughts into a prayer. For example:

Lord God, forgive us for the way we waste energy and use up what cannot be replaced. Help us to limit harmful changes in the environment. Help us not to live for today with no thought for tomorrow. Help us to handle the world with care and respect, for our own sake and for the children in the next generation. Amen

6. In a church school, a statement of belief may be important. The simple one used at baptisms may be appropriate, or you could use the version below, which is the author's own wording.

We believe and trust in God the Father who made the world.
We believe and trust in his Son Jesus Christ, who redeemed the world.

We believe and trust in his Holy Spirit, who gives life to the people of God.
We believe and trust in one God, Father, Son and Holy Spirit.

7. Younger children could be given an apple, pear or banana shape on which to write a prayer. Their prayer could refer either to the fruit or to anything they would like to give thanks for. The options could be expanded to include other harvest items, such as a loaf of bread.

Curriculum link: Citizenship

There is a clear opportunity to link the harvest theme with a greater understanding of global citizenship—our relationship with the wider world community.

Ideas for exploring the theme

1. For information about how charities can help bridge the hunger gap, contact charities such as Christian Aid, Tearfund, Oxfam, or Send a Cow. Children could research a particular charity and report back. Your school may wish to consider supporting a particular charity for a term, as a way of responding to the needs the children have detected. Fundraising in order to show your care and concern can be great fun and can help a class or whole school to bond.

2. Ask children to write down what they think is the biggest problem in the world today, and then list their answers for a discussion. What can be done about these problems?

3. Ask the children to investigate, or even bake, bread from different parts of the world, and present their findings. You could start them off with some examples—larger supermarkets stock a surprising variety. Ask children to bring in labels so that they gain an increasing understanding of where our food comes from. The labels could be mounted round the edge of a world map, increasing the children's

geographical knowledge. Alternatively, you could focus on fruit and create a class fruit salad using a variety from home and abroad, or bake a cake or some buns as a class, recording where the ingredients come from. Record the process with a digital camera to show in assembly.

4. Many shops now stock products labelled as part of a Fair Trade scheme, which is well worth exploring and explaining. Here are some key statements you could present in an assembly, or as a questions-and-answers interview:

⊙ One billion people live in poverty. Many of them could improve their lives if it were not for the unfair rules of the world trade system.

⊙ The 'developed world' seems to take from poor people to give to rich companies and rich countries. These companies make big profits. The governments from many rich countries have the power to bully poor countries into accepting trade rules to keep them poor.

⊙ One way to make a difference is to support Fair Trade and buy products from which more of the profit gets back to the producers in poor countries.

⊙ At the beginning of this century, Fair Trade began to grow. During 2001, total Fair Trade sales leapt by 40 per cent. Bananas provided the most popular increase in sales, going up by 83 per cent. British people spent £43 million on Fair Trade products—the same as £1.45 every second. It's a great way to help and to enjoy tasty food at the same time.

⊙ Products with the Fairtrade mark are available in supermarkets and Fair Trade shops. Here are some of them (*hold up packets and read out the names*). Remember to look out for the Fairtrade marks like these if you want to be sure the food producers are getting a better deal. Even buying one Fair Trade item each time you shop will make a huge difference.

Another way of using this information (and any more that you can gain from packets and leaflets) is to encourage the children to write an advert or radio jingle. This could lead to some research into which foods are harvested in other countries and transported to us. A contrast could be reported between harvest time here and in a particular country such as Ethiopia or India.

The children could be given information on Fair Trade and asked to find out more before deciding how to make a presentation for an audience, perhaps of parents (see Worksheet 5, which can be downloaded free of charge from the 'Books and resources' section of the *Barnabas* website, www.barnabasinschools.org.uk).

Curriculum link: Literacy

Poetry

Performance is an important part of any Literacy strategy. As part of an assembly, learning all or part of a poem for a presentation is useful for developing memory and often forms part of people's favourite recalled moments of life at school. There are many published poems about harvest to choose from, both contemporary and classic. Alternatively, you could write your own, using a haiku or tanka to capture a scene or one moment in time, for example:

The sunflower grew
Towering over other plants
A garden giant

You could try writing a four-verse poem based on the four seasons. It could be a comparison of the same scene at different times of the year. The format could be a set of haikus (called a renga). Alternatively, you might like to try a rap set against a background of an electronic keyboard or live sounds from children (slap, slap, clap or boom, boom, char... and so on). Here's one you might like to try. Put four stresses on each line to mark the rhythm.

Plump potatoes, long green beans,
The juiciest apples you've ever seen;
Crunchy carrots, orangey red,
Cut that corn: we need flour for our bread.

Thank you to the farmers; thank you for the rain,
Thank you that the harvest is gathered in again.

It's been good fun playing in the sun,
The crops just keep on growing until the harvest's done.
Rhubarb in the garden; some think it's far too sour,
Plums hang ready, oh so sweet, swelling by the hour.

Thank you to the farmers; thank you for the rain,
Thank you that the harvest is gathered in again.

The children could practise their handwriting skills by copying lines of a published poem or copying out their own, adding a decorated border. Alternatively, the poem could be typed up and a border or clip art chosen as a design task.

Wordsearches

Use the wordsearch on Worksheet 6, which can be downloaded free of charge from the 'Books and resources' section of the *Barnabas* website, www.barnabasinschools.org.uk. Alternatively, create your own on squared paper. Traditionally, wordsearches are done all in capital letters, but you can make this choice.

Visit the website http://puzzlemaker.school.discovery.com. Here, you can type in your choice of words and it will create a wordsearch for you.

Curriculum link: Art

Ideas for exploring the theme

1. Pressed flowers and leaves can be mounted on strips of thin card as bookmarks. If laminated, they last longer and make splendid gifts.

2. Using the story of creation in the Bible (Genesis 1:1—2:4), create pictures for each of the stages of creation.

3. Look at the work of artists such as Turner and Constable for examples of landscape, skyscape and depiction of light. Children could study a particular painting in detail and report back, experimenting with the technique.

4. Look at the work of Giuseppe Acrimboldo, the 16th-century Italian artist who painted heads made up of all sorts of objects, including fruit, vegetables and plants. It is fun to identify all the different things to eat in his pictures. He also designed costumes for royalty and was particularly popular with the emperors in Austria. You could try designing a portrait using this unusual starting point.

5. Design a set of stamps on an autumn or harvest theme.

6. Encourage children in their observation of drawing and still-life work using fruits and vegetables.

7. Use half an apple, a hard pear or an onion as print blocks.

Other curriculum links

Mathematics

Count the seeds inside different fruits and turn the data into a graph.

Science

Play odd-one-out with pictures, objects or words. Can the children give a reason for their choice?

Music

Listen to and reflect on classical music such as *The Love of Three Oranges* by Prokofiev (this is an interesting story to dramatize), 'Till Eulenspiegel' by Richard Strauss, or 'What a wonderful world' by Louis Armstrong. Alternatively, compose your own sound collection to create a market scene with conversation, traders' calls, footsteps, dogs barking and so on.

Saints

Saints can be divided into three categories. First of all, there are Jesus' first disciples and apostles, who were the first people to take the gospel to the known world. Second, there are those Christians who, down the centuries, have led holy lives, and, third, there are all those who would count themselves among the people of God as modern-day followers of Jesus Christ.

Curriculum link: RE

Ideas for exploring the theme

1. Research the patron saints of the British Isles—St Andrew, St George, St Patrick and St David. If there is a church named after one of these saints in your area, the minister may be able to help with your research.

2. Explore people who the children regard as special and find out why they admire them. They could include people who help us, family, friends, and people in the local community. Add in the religious aspect and remind children of possible definitions for the word 'saint'—for example, people who do what would please God, such as building a fairer world or serving others, as Jesus would have done. Who comes to mind as a good example? Real 'saints in the making' don't draw attention to themselves, so they could be people nearby. Remind children what Jesus taught us about being a neighbour in the story of the good Samaritan (Luke 10:25–37).

3. Research the life of Mother Teresa and the impact she made, not just on those with whom she worked, but also on people who never met her.

4. Use the material about different saints in *Stories of Everyday Saints* by Veronica Heley (BRF).

Curriculum link: PSHE and Citizenship

Ideas for exploring the theme

1. There is lot of emphasis in our world on celebrity. Older children could explore how useful this emphasis is. For example, are our football heroes or pop stars suitable role models? Does fame itself cause some people to behave badly or crack under the pressure? The children could even consider the role of the royal family, and think about how fair it is to expect people in this position to be good examples, or to avoid the pressures of life in their possessions and relationships. Also, is it fair to expect perfection from religious people who try harder than some to do what they feel is right?

2. Find out as much as you can about Jesus' disciples. Were they a suitable group for the job? What qualities do you think they would have needed? You could write a job description for the ones you know most about. What might an advert have looked like if Jesus had wanted to interview people? Why are there no women on the list? (He did have women among his close followers, but not among those he trained and sent out as his twelve closest disciples.) Many of these first disciples and followers of Jesus became the saints we honour today. In so many ways, they were a very ordinary group of people, but they had many practical skills. If you were trying to make sure your work would carry on after you were gone, what kinds of people would you choose to do it? What skills would they have?

3. Consider the idea of a dream football team. Imagine you could choose players from any team, whatever the cost. Who would you choose to play in goal, in defence, up front, or on the wing? What types of personalities would you need? How would you get the mix of skills you need? What is the role of the head coach? How would you mould them into a team in time for their first game? This is often the role that a country's manager has to play when he is allowed to choose a team.

4. Talk about what you think Jesus would want to change in the world today.

Curriculum link: Literacy

Ideas for exploring the theme

1. Explore ways of sending messages, such as Morse code, sending a text message, faxing, e-mails, or semaphore. These could all be demonstrated in class or in assembly.

Other examples, not so easy to perform but worth explaining, might be carrier pigeons and their role in war time, telegrams, satellite, and the development of the postal service from the Victorian period till now. Children could use the internet to research these methods and write a non-chronological report.

2. Write an acrostic that explains what a saint is.

3. Write a performance poem to explain the idea that everybody who follows Jesus, using him as their example, can be regarded as a saint in the making—for example:

You don't have to be a hero,
You don't have to learn to fight;
All you need is to follow Jesus
And trust in his power and might.

You don't have to be great or famous,
You don't have to be clever or rich,
Just listen to the words of Jesus—
Obey what he came down to teach.

God wants you to know that you're special,
Wants you to treat others that way too;
When you get to a tricky decision, think,
'Now what would Jesus do?'

Take every chance that you're given
To help those you find in need,
Then you're in step with the saints in heaven
And following Jesus indeed.

Remembrance

The theme of remembrance focuses both on the importance of remembering those involved in war and on the history of God's people's as a chosen nation.

Curriculum link: RE

Match the boxes

The word 'holiday' derives from 'holy day', stemming from the days when time off work or school was based around Christian festivals. With the approach of Advent, the start of the Christian year, consider the important festivals that are celebrated to tell the story of the life of Jesus. Download Worksheet 7 free of charge from the 'Books and resources' section of the Barnabas website, www.barnabasinschools.org.uk. Ask the children to cut out the boxes and then match the time of the Christian year with the correct event and correct month.

Discuss with the children the importance of remembering special events. What other events do they think we should mark? For example, should we now include the main festivals of other major religions, such as Passover, Hannukah, Diwali, Eid-al-Fitr or Baisakhi? Should we include days that are of historical importance, such as Trafalgar Day, St George's Day, Shakespeare's birthday, Remembrance Day, Armistice Day, VE Day and VJ Day? Or should we be celebrating more Christian holy days, such as Epiphany and Ascension Day?

Remembering what God has done

In the Bible, the word 'remember' is very important. People who believe in God find it helpful to reflect on what God has done in the past as a signpost to his reliability and faithfulness for the present. Read the Bible passages below and ask the children what the key words or images are in the passage to help people remember what God has done. What words or images do we use to remember things that have been done as a mark of care for us?

Listen, Israel! The Lord our God is the only true God! So love the Lord your God with all your heart, soul, and strength. Memorize his laws and tell them to your children over and over again. Talk about them all the time, whether you're at home or walking along the road or going to bed at night, or getting up in the morning. Write down copies and tie them to your wrists and foreheads to help you obey them. Write these laws on the door frames of your homes and on your town gates.

DEUTERONOMY 6:4–9

When I send clouds over the earth, and a rainbow appears in the sky, I will remember my promise to you and to all other living creatures. Never again will I let floodwaters destroy all life. When I see the rainbow in the sky, I will always remember the promise that I have made to every living creature. The rainbow will be the sign of that solemn promise.

GENESIS 9:14–17

Remember the solemn promise you made to Abraham, Isaac, and Jacob. You promised that some day they would have as many descendants as there are stars in the sky and that you would give them land.

EXODUS 32:13

Here is the new agreement that I, the Lord, will make with the people of Israel: 'I will write my laws on their hearts and minds.

I will be their God, and they will be my people. No longer will they have to teach one another to obey me. I, the Lord, promise that all of them will obey me, ordinary people and rulers alike. I will forgive their sins and forget the evil things they have done.'
JEREMIAH 31:33–34

Jesus took some bread in his hands. Then after he had given thanks, he broke it and said, 'This is my body, which is given for you. Eat this and remember me.' After the meal, Jesus took a cup of wine in his hands and said, 'This is my blood, and with it God makes his new agreement with you. Drink this and remember me.'
1 CORINTHIANS 11:23b–25

'Jesus isn't here! He has been raised from death. Remember that while he was still in Galilee, he told you, "The Son of Man will be handed over to sinners who will nail him to a cross. But three days later he will rise to life."' Then they remembered what Jesus had said.
LUKE 24:6–8

Using symbols for remembrance

For many people, especially those involved in war, remembering can be a painful process. With older children, discuss why people might have difficulty in forgiving or forgetting war-time experiences. The poppy is a symbol of war that carries with it layers of understanding. Discuss how different people might use this symbol to remember in different ways.

What other symbols help us to remember? For example, Christian symbols include the cross, bread and wine, water and light. For many families who have suffered bereavement, remembering is a mixture of sadness and memories. What symbols might people use to remember someone who has died?

Curriculum link: Citizenship

1. Make a list of the days that are important in our country. Which of these days have become important because someone tried to change the way we live? If a significant number of people wish to change the way society works, how should they go about bringing change? How can they make their views known? Is vandalism or violence ever an appropriate way to make your voice heard?

Tease out the concept of democracy: voting for local government representatives, access to politicians at local level, public campaigns such as Make Poverty History, the way that councils work at local, county and regional level through to Parliament itself. You could invite someone from one of these bodies to talk to the children or be interviewed by them. Many schools have representatives of these local councils as Governors and children relish the opportunity to let these people know their views on their local facilities and to quiz them on how decisions are made about planning for parks and housing. Many schools now have a School Council, with representatives from each class who discuss improvements to the school and carry views back and forth between the class and Council.

2. Discuss the children's views on people who are celebrated as role models in our society. What qualities do they admire in them? What about people with natural talent who have trained hard to extend their abilities, such as sports stars or record breakers? What about people who have become famous because they entertain us in some way? Why are superheroes from comic books and films so popular? What qualities do we admire in them?

Curriculum link: Literacy

Exploring the Gunpowder Plot

1. Create a list poem using names of fireworks (real or invented). You can add gasps and oohs! You could present this poem linked to the musical ideas (see page 148) as a joint Literacy/Music composition.

2. Write in the first person from the viewpoint of someone in the gunpowder plot narrative: you could be Guy being discovered, or one of the investigators writing a report on how you were the one to capture Guy. You could write a report for the *London Times*. Use persuasive writing to communicate why you think you are doing the right thing in this event.

3. Research and write a balanced report on the views of both Catholics and Protestants at the time of the gunpowder plot. This could develop into a debate about the plot.

4. Research and role-play the characters involved in the gunpowder plot. You might want to dramatize the search of the Parliament building, but not necessarily the torture of Guy!

5. Write a set of rules for using candles in the classroom or at home.

6. Learn the famous 'Remember, remember' rhyme and present it as a choral poem (see Worksheet 1, which can be downloaded free of charge from the 'Books and resources' section of the *Barnabas* website, www.barnabasinschools.org.uk).

Exploring historical and contemporary heroes

1. Research people who have become famous because of what they have done (or do), such as Christopher Columbus, St Francis of Assisi, Grace Darling, Colin Jackson or David Beckham. *The Guinness Book of Records* is a goldmine of information about amazing and unusual people.

2. Write your own story based on a hero who did something amazing. It could be a fictional superhero or someone in real life who, when faced with the need for bravery, found extra strength and courage. For example, it could be a person who saved someone from a fire, a schoolchild who used his or her knowledge of first aid to help someone in difficulty, or someone who trained for a dangerous job, such as a fire fighter or member of a lifeboat crew.

3. Use anthologies of war poems, such as in the Pelican series, or *In Time of War* (edited by Anne Harvey in association with The Imperial War Museum), to explore the theme of remembrance.

Curriculum link: Art

1. Draw Guy Fawkes laying the gunpowder, hiding in the cellar or being captured.

2. Draw fireworks, using chalks on black paper or with wax on white, highlighted with wax-resist dye.

3. Make a painting of poppies and use them as part of a display about remembering those involved in war. Research the artist Georgia O'Keeffe, who is known for her vivid painting of poppies.

Curriculum link: Music

Listen to extracts from Handel's *Music for the Royal Fireworks*. Which fireworks match with the musical extracts? Use voices and experiment with instruments to see which are suitable for a rocket, a Catherine wheel, a Roman fountain and so on. You might find that you need a background sound pattern running to connect the individual sounds. You could play the music as a stimulus or to accompany the drawing of fireworks.

Curriculum link: ICT

1. Research the story of Guy Fawkes on the internet. Cut and paste relevant information into a Word document, then edit to ensure that it is presented in your own words. Turn your research into an article, making sure that you match the presentation and language you use for the piece to your intended audience.

2. Using the internet, research war poems and archive material on British involvement in war. The BBC has collated a lot of material. The websites of the Royal British Legion and the Imperial War Museum are also well worth exploring.

3. Explore the internet to find out about charities involved in rescue, such as the Royal National Lifeboat Institute.

Curriculum link: Science

Light and shadows

Very few of us ever experience what it is like when there is absolutely no light, but if any of the children have camped in a forest or meadow away from houses, they might have some idea. Has anyone ever been down a mine? Talk about the fact that there needs to be a light source in order for us to see. We see because light travels into our eyes. In fact, light travels faster than anything else we know.

Nowadays we are used to having street lighting, rather than relying on lanterns and moonlight to see at night. Discuss light pollution and energy wastage with the children. Our eyes are able to adapt to less light than usual. Try reading the same page in places with different amounts of light. How long does it take until you are 'ready' to read the words in the darker areas? Did you know that Jewish people say that night has fallen when they can no longer tell the difference between a black and white thread?

Use a lantern or a torch to investigate shadows. Think about how people in Tudor and Stuart times told the time. For example, did they use church clocks or sundials? Did they calculate the time by looking at the position of the sun or moon?

Light facts

Research interesting facts about light. Here are some to start you off:

- ☼ The light from a star left that star millions of years ago (perhaps at a time when dinosaurs roamed the earth).
- ☼ Light from the sun takes eight and a half minutes to reach us.
- ☼ Light from the nearest star beyond our sun takes just over four years to reach us.
- ☼ Some of the stars we see may no longer exist.

Light and the human eye

Explain about the two types of cells in the eye that detect light: rods and cones. Rods need far less light and cannot detect colour. Cones can detect colour, but only work in bright light. Why is it that we can see fireworks clearly even in the dark? Discuss with a partner what life would be like if our eyes could only see in black and white. What would life be like if we did not have cone cells in our eyes?

Light and the animal kingdom

Find out about animals that give out natural light in the form of bioluminescence. How do animals that live underground cope without access to light? How have animals adapted that live in the deep ocean, far from light sources?

Curriculum link: Design and Technology

Design a lantern for a firework party. Consider all the safety aspects and choose materials with care. Will it be easy to light? You could link this project to research into what Guy Fawkes' lantern looked like (the original is in the Ashmolean Museum in Oxford: see www.ashmolean.org/ash/objectofmonth/2002-11/theobject.htm). The lantern is made of two cylinders, one inside the other. The outer cylinder had a window made of horn, through which the candle inside could shine. The inner cylinder could slide across to hide the light completely.

Advent

Curriculum link: RE

1. Explore different Christmas customs, such as the origins of the Christmas crib with its link to St Francis, and discuss how they relate back to the original story. This exploration of customs could be linked to a topic on the Tudors or Victorians.

2. Research how Christmas is celebrated around the world. Make a list of customs that are very different from ours, and some that are similar or the same. How do different customs relate to the original Christmas story?

Curriculum link: Citizenship

Explore the word 'peace' and what we mean by the concept of peace. Use speech bubbles to write down suggestions of how the word is used. For example, 'For goodness' sake, settle down. I need some peace and quiet'; 'Isn't it peaceful on this beach?'; 'Why can't you make peace with each other?'; 'There doesn't seem to be much hope of the countries making peace.' Discuss the idea that most people prefer to live peaceably. How can peaceful living be achieved in different situations? Are there times when it would be impossible?

Curriculum link: Literacy

1. Write a narrative of the Christmas story told from different viewpoints. The Advent crown could be a suitable starting point for writing from the point of view of individuals or groups who have played a key role in God's plans, such as:

- The patriarchs
- The prophets
- John the Baptist
- Mary
- Jesus

Alternatively, the characters could include the innkeeper, Joseph, the shepherds, the donkey or even the star. This could link to preparation work in Literacy. (See Appendix Two on page 164 for ideas linking Literacy to an Advent assembly.)

2. Using one of the main characters, make an acrostic of other people involved in the Christmas story. For example, a Christmas acrostic for 'Jesus' could be:

Joseph: agreed that he and Mary should be married.
Emperor Augustus: decreed that everyone should return to their home town so that their name could be listed in the record books.
Shepherds: were told by angels that Jesus had been born.
Us: Emmanuel means 'God with us'.
Saviour: Jesus is the Saviour of the world.

3. Tell Tolstoy's story of Papa Panov, who dreamt that Jesus himself would visit. Papa Panov had fallen asleep while reading the Bible story about the birth of Jesus. Throughout Christmas Day, he expected Jesus to arrive. While he waited for Jesus to come, he welcomed a variety of people into his home and helped each person in some way. At the end of the day, Papa Panov felt disappointed that Jesus hadn't visited, but as he drifted off to sleep that evening, he heard Jesus saying how pleased he was that Papa Panov had helped so many visitors by attending to their basic needs. In this way, Papa Panov had fulfilled Jesus' words in Matthew 25:40 that what we do for others, we do for God himself.

The story could be dramatized for an assembly or presentation to parents. It could also be used for hot-seating the thoughts of the characters and to freeze-frame key moments chosen by the children. Use a digital camera to photograph the freeze-frames and use them for further discussion, display or adding captions.

4. Think of the things that help us to know that Christmas is coming. The resulting list poem might include:

⚙ Christmas songs and carols are playing in every shop.
⚙ Dad asks, 'Who's had the Sellotape?'
⚙ The TV guides last two weeks instead of one.
⚙ Everyone asks, 'Will it snow this Christmas?'
⚙ Brussels sprouts go on sale in the supermarket.
⚙ Every pop star wants the Christmas number one.
⚙ Sales have already started.
⚙ People are loaded down with shopping bags.
⚙ Every other advert on TV is for perfume.
⚙ Neighbours compete for the 'most lights on a house' prize.

What other things can you think of?

5. Compile an Advent list poem, using as many words as you can think of for each letter of the alphabet. Starting with 1 December, turn your list into an Advent calendar, using one of the following ideas.

⚙ Design a circular Advent calendar with 24 segments, and copy your list into the segments. Cut out a second circle from paper, the same size as the first, with one segment cut away to fit over the calendar. Decorate the front of the second circle with a Christmas scene, and fix it over the first with a split-pin fastener. The second circle becomes a wheel to reveal the Advent list, one slot at a time.
⚙ The Advent list could be spiral-bound into an Advent book, turning the pages to reveal each new day. The list could be organized alphabetically or in a random order.

✪ Your Advent calendar could be turned into a giant display piece for the classroom, with each idea being illustrated and hung from pegs across the classroom or on a giant tree shape. The list can be revealed either by unpeeling paper covering each picture or by taking each idea out of an envelope.

In order to make the calendar work for the school timespan, place just enough items on the calendar to get you from the beginning of December until the end of term. Finish with the baby in the stable.

6. Ask the children to write a list poem based on the concept of contrasting pairs in Isaiah 11:6–7. More able children could begin the poem with obvious matches and gradually move to those that are less comfortable, then to those matches that could only come about with help from God. Try to come up with a strong last line such as 'Love your enemies and those you hate, just as Jesus said!' or 'Person with person; nation with nation; working together in harmony and peace.'

7. Role-play typical situations in school that lead to arguments, and try different ways of resolving them, such as adult intervention, asking friends to help, finding your own solution and so on.

8. Construct a poem to be performed as choral speech, using different colours that might feature in the Christmas story. Give a limited amount of structure for children to work with, such as the first words of the lines:

Silver the star…
Green was…
Gold for…

Use a refrain such as:

Colours of Christmas,
Lighting the way,
Show us the Saviour
We welcome today.

Use the 'Sans Day Carol' ('The holly bears a berry') to explore the idea of Christmas colours. Extend it to explain how the Christian year is marked in many churches with different colours for different seasons. The colours of the church are:

- Advent: purple
- Christmas: white or gold
- Epiphany and Candlemas: white or gold
- Lent: purple
- Palm Sunday: red
- Maundy Thursday: white
- Good Friday: a bare church with no ornaments or furnishings
- Easter Day: white or gold
- Ascension Day: white or gold
- Pentecost: red
- Trinity Sunday: white
- Ordinary times: green
- All Saints: white or gold

Colours of Christmas

This is an example of a completed poem that could be used for your choral speech or as a stimulus for the children to write their own.

Silver the star that led to the stable with radiant glow,
Green was the hay that cradled the baby long, long ago,
Gold were the offerings the wise men came to bring
To the child in the manger, proclaiming him king.

Colours of Christmas,
Lighting the way,
Show us the Saviour
We welcome today.

Brown for the oxen sharing their shelter that cold winter's night,
Yellow the flame that lit up the scene with shadowy light,
White for the lambs watched by young shepherd boys
When the angels appeared with their message of joy.

Colours of Christmas,
Lighting the way,
Show us the Saviour
We welcome today.

What can we give the babe in the manger, the child become king?
Bring him our hearts and offer the praises we sing.
Worship and reverence we show to him now—
At the name of Christ Jesus all people will bow.

Colours of Christmas,
Lighting the way,
Show us the Saviour
We welcome today.
MARTIN COX

Curriculum link: Art

1. Use the words in Isaiah 11:6–9 as a stimulus for art. You may need to provide templates of pictures of animals for the children to copy. Discuss whether the animals might share the same bed or food. What other unlikely pairs can the children think of? Could a mouse ride on the back of a cat? Use the words in Isaiah 2:3–5 to explore the concept of peace. You could modernize the words used for weapons and tools.

The Lord will teach us his Law from Jerusalem, and we will obey him. He will settle arguments between nations. They will beat their swords and their spears into rakes and shovels; they will never make war or attack one another. People of Israel, let's live by the light of the Lord.

ISAIAH 2:3b–5

2. Experiment with different colours to explore the idea of complementary and contrasting colours on a colour wheel. Which colours tend to create a peaceful mood and which are more challenging?

3. Design a stained-glass window on the Advent theme. Think about the people in the Bible who were involved in the first Christmas story, or who got ready for Jesus' arrival. Think about symbols that could be used to show that we are getting ready to celebrate the birth of Jesus. Collect Christmas cards in a stained-glass window style to use as examples.

4. For many people, a star is an important Christmas symbol, as it pointed the way for the wise men to travel to see Jesus. Star templates can lead to many art ideas, such as mobiles, tessellation, printing and collage.

5. Use the angels featured in the Christmas story as a starting point for both 2D and 3D work.

6. Design postage stamps depicting different parts of the Christmas story.

7. Make your own Christmas cards, gift tags, wrapping paper or gift bags and talk about the idea of giving.

Curriculum link: Numeracy

1. Draw a scale map of the Holy Land at the time of Jesus. Work out distances, such as the journey from Nazareth to Bethlehem, and the typical journey that people would have made from Nazareth to visit the temple in Jerusalem. You could extend this activity with other references to places where Jesus travelled, such as from Lake Galilee to Jerusalem.

2. Invent mathematical questions based on the song 'The twelve days of Christmas'. For example:

● How many rings were given by the ninth day?
● How many presents were given on the twelfth day?
● How many presents were given all together?
● How many of the presents were living things?
● How many animals were given as presents on the tenth day?

3. Ask the children to imagine they are the person receiving all the presents. Would they be grateful or ungrateful? What sort of mess and chaos might ensue? The children could write a letter asking the sender to stop, or even record both voices in a phone call between the two parties.

4. Find a recipe for a Christmas cake or mince pies and ask the children to work out the ratios for half the quantity, three times, or even two and a half times the amount of ingredients.

5. Conduct a paper chain investigation. Decide on a limited amount of paper, such as two (different coloured) sheets of A4 paper, and challenge small groups to make the longest paper chain they can in a limited time. You could give different groups the same tools (glue stick, PVA, stapler, a metre of sticky tape and so on) or different ones.

Curriculum link: History

Discuss the idea of a census and its purpose both in Roman times and now. Then access the internet for data on census information gathered in your area or national statistics about Britain today.

Curriculum link: ICT

1. Make an Advent fun book to include puzzles such as word-searches, cracker jokes, Christmas quizzes and poems to perform.

2. Devise a crossword grid using one of the following methods.

- List the answers, which then need to be fitted correctly into the grid from a given starting letter.
- Give clues for each word and put a few letters in place on the grid to help with the correct answers.
- Work out a number code for each letter of the alphabet and then list the answers using only the number code. Place a few numbers on the grid to help identify which letter goes with which number.

A sample grid might be:

Mary
Advent
Sheep
Shepherd
John
Herod
Joseph
Donkey
Angel
Inn

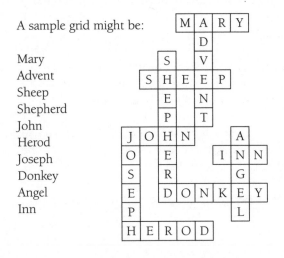

PART THREE

Appendices

—————— **Appendix One** ——————

National Curriculum: index of related QCA units

This index is correct at the time of going to press. Please also refer to the Non-Strategy National Framework for RE for further related units, and the Dfes Standards website, www.standards.dfes.gov.uk, for up-to-date revisions.

Harvest

RE Unit RA: What are harvest festivals?
RE Unit 2B: Why did Jesus tell stories?
Science Unit 1B: Growing plants
Science Unit 2B: Plants and animals in the local environment
Science Unit 3B: Helping plants grow well
Science Unit 4B: Habitats
Science Unit 5B: Life cycles
Science Unit 6A: Interdependence and adaptation
DT Unit 1C: Eat more fruit and vegetables
DT Unit 3B: Sandwich snacks
DT Unit 5B: Bread
DT Unit 5D: Biscuits

Saints

RE Unit RB: Who were the friends of Jesus?
RE Unit 1B: What does it mean to belong in Christianity?
RE Unit 2B: Why did Jesus tell stories?
RE Unit 3E: What is faith and what difference does it make?
RE Unit 5D: How do the beliefs of Christians influence their actions?
History Unit 20: What can we learn about recent history from studying the life of a famous person?

Remembrance

RE Unit 3A: What do signs and symbols mean in religion?
Citizenship Unit 1:   Taking Part
Citizenship Unit 8:   How do rules and laws affect me?
Citizenship Unit 10: Local democracy
History Unit 17:   What are we remembering on Remembrance Day?

Advent

RE Unit 5D: How do the beliefs of Christians influence their actions?
Science Unit 1D: Light and dark
Science Unit 3F: Light and shadows
Science Unit 6F: How we see things

Appendix Two

Literacy links for an Advent assembly

Here is a list of possibilities for Literacy links that could lead to your own set of assemblies in Advent, prepared by one or more classes. The 'T' references are to the Text level objectives in the current National Literacy Strategy document.

Year 1

T5:   describe story settings and incidents and relate them to own experience/that of others.

T7:   re-enact stories in a variety of ways (puppets, dolls, the nativity play…).

T9:   write about events in personal experience and link to known stories (birth of a baby).

T11: make a simple picture storybook with sentences modelled on text conventions.

T14: write captions for their own work, e.g. tell part of the story each for a class book.

Year 2

T3:   develop awareness of the difference between spoken and written language: use formal story elements in retelling and notice the difference when it is acted out.

T4: understand time and relationships in stories—what happened when: order a muddled sequence of events about Jesus' birth

T5: identify reasons why things happen linked to plot: why was Jesus born in a stable?

T6: discuss familiar story themes and link to experience: journeys, riding a donkey

T11: use the language of time to sequence events—link to T4 (improve the given sequence or use as a model)

T12: use simple poetry structures and substitute own lines, e.g. an acrostic such as STAR

Year 3

T11: write a description in the style of a familiar story

T13: write a poem based on the senses, e.g. describe the sights and smells of the stable

T15: write a short play script based on one's reading and oral work

Year 4

T2: identify characteristics of key characters in a narrative

T3/4: map out the chronology of the story from the Bible text or a quality retelling

T11: write a character sketch focusing on small details to evoke sympathy or dislike

T13: write a play script using a known story as a basis

T14: write a poem based on imagined experience, experimenting with powerful verbs

T24: write a newspaper-style report, e.g. about an incident in a story

Year 5

T15: write new scenes or characters into a story
T16: convey feelings/reflections in a poem (explain how you reacted/felt as Mary or Joseph)
T18: write own play script or annotate a given one for performance
T24: write a news report/recount of a historical event

Year 6

T2: take account of narrative viewpoint
T6: produce a modern retelling
T8: summarize a passage, chapter or given text in a specific number of words
T9: prepare a short section of the story as a script with directions
T10: write a poem using personification—be the star, the stable, an animal...
T14: write a diary/journal as part of biographical/autobiographical writing
T16: journalistic writing

— Appendix Three —

Index of songs and music

Harvest

Songs

All the nations of the earth (*Come and Praise* 14)
All things bright and beautiful (*Come and Praise* 3; *Kidsource* 8)
Autumn days (*Come and Praise* 4)
Cauliflowers fluffy (*Harlequin*)
Come, you thankful people, come (*Hymns Old and New* 101)
God created them all (*Songs for Every Day*—Out of the Ark)
God is love, his the care (*Come and Praise* 36)
Harvest hymn (*Songs for Every Occasion*—Out of the Ark)
Harvest samba (*Songs for Every Occasion*—Out of the Ark)
Harvest song (*Songs for Every Season*—Out of the Ark)
Have you heard the raindrops? (*Come and Praise* 2; *Kidsource* 99)
I listen (*Come and Praise* 60)
He's got the whole world in his hands (*Come and Praise* 19)
Jesus' love is very wonderful (*Kidsource* 208)
Lord of the harvest (*Come and Praise* 133)
My God is so big (*Kidsource* 255)
Pears and apples (*Come and Praise* 135)
Thank you, Lord (*Come and Praise* 32)
Think of a world without any flowers (*Come and Praise* 17)
We plough the fields (*Hymns Old and New* 534)
When I needed a neighbour (*Come and Praise* 65)
Who put the colours in the rainbow? (*Come and Praise* 12; *Kidsource* 386)
Who's the king of the jungle? (*Kidsource* 388)

Music

The circle of life (from *The Lion King*)
The four seasons (Vivaldi)
What a wonderful world (Louis Armstrong or Alison Moyet)
Symphony No. 6: Pastoral (Beethoven)
The lark ascending (Vaughan-Williams)
On hearing the first cuckoo of spring (Delius)
The love of three oranges (Prokofiev)
Till Eulenspiegel (Richard Strauss)

Saints

Songs

All the nations of the earth (*Come and Praise* 14)
All things bright and beautiful (*Come and Praise* 3)
Colours of day (*Come and Praise* 55)
Count your blessings (*Songs for Every Occasion*—Out of the Ark)
For all the saints (*Hymns Old and New* 134)
For I'm building a people of power (*Kidsource* 61)
Give me oil in my lamp (*Come and Praise* 43)
God is love, his the care (*Come and Praise* 36)
God's people aren't super brave superheroes (*Kidsource* 86)
He made me (*Come and Praise* 18)
He'll be there (*Songs for Every Assembly*—Out of the Ark)
He's got the whole world in his hands (*Come and Praise* 19)
Jesus' love is very wonderful (*Kidsource* 208)
Make me a channel of your peace (*Come and Praise* 147; *Kidsource* 248)
My God is so big (*Kidsource* 255)
One more step (*Come and Praise* 47; *Kidsource* 273)
Our Father (*Come and Praise* 51)
Peter and John went to pray (*Kidsource* 281)

Spirit of God (*Come and Praise* 63)

Thank you, Jesus, thank you, Lord (*Kidsource* 313)

Thank you, Lord (*Come and Praise* 32)

When a knight won his spurs (*Come and Praise* 50; *Kidsource* 371)

When I needed a neighbour (*Come and Praise* 65)

When I survey the wondrous cross (*Hymns Old and New* 549)

Remembrance

Songs

Make me a channel of your peace (*Come and Praise* 147; *Kidsource* 248)

Remember (see Worksheet 2, which can be downloaded free of charge from the 'Books and resources' section of the *Barnabas* website, www.barnabasinschools.org.uk)

We will remember (*Songs for Every Occasion*—Out of the Ark)

Music

Dambusters March (Eric Coates)

'Nimrod' from *Enigma Variations* (Edward Elgar)

Music for the Royal Fireworks (George Frederick Handel)

Spitfire Prelude and Fugue (William Walton)

War-time songs

Advent

Songs

Advent round (see Worksheet 8, which can be downloaded free of charge from the 'Books and resources' section of the *Barnabas* website, www.barnabasinschools.org.uk)

At the name of Jesus (*Come and Praise* 58)

Christmas time is here (Advent time…) (*Come and Praise* 127)

He came down that we might have love (*World Praise* 27: number varies according to edition)

He's got the whole world in his hands (*Come and Praise* 19)

I've got peace like a river (*Come and Praise* 143)

Jesus' love is very wonderful (*Kidsource* 208)

King of kings and Lord of lords (*Carol Praise* 154; *The Source* 307)

Candle in the window (Light a candle) (*Come and Praise* 118)

Like a candle flame (*The Source* 322)

O little town of Bethlehem (*Carol Praise* 213; *Sing Nowell*)

On Jordan's bank (*Carol Praise* 226)

Peace is flowing (*Come and Praise* 144)

Peace, perfect peace (*Come and Praise* 53)

Spirit of peace (*Come and Praise* 85)

The angel Gabriel from heaven came (*Carol Praise* 286; *Merrily to Bethlehem* 2)

The king of love my shepherd is (*Come and Praise* 54)

The servant king (*Kidsource* 62; *Carol Praise* 91)

Together (*Songs for Every Assembly*—Out of the Ark)

When I needed a neighbour (*Come and Praise* 65)

While shepherds watched (*Carol Praise* 341; *Sing Nowell*)

Who's the king of the jungle? (*Kidsource* 388; *Songs of Fellowship for Kids* 184)

Working together (*Every Colour under the Sun* 37)

Music

Coronation music, such as:

 Messiah, Part 1 (George Frederick Handel)

 Zadok the Priest (George Frederick Handel)

 Crown Imperial/Orb and Sceptre (William Walton)

Index of Bible passages

Speech bubble template

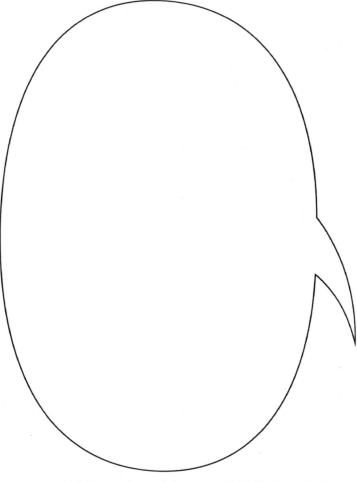

Bibliography

Music

Come and Praise, ed. Geoffrey Marshall-Taylor (BBC)
Junior Praise (Collins)
Kidsource, ed. Capt. Alan Price (Kevin Mayhew)
The Source (Kevin Mayhew)
Harlequin (A&C Black)
Sing Nowell (A&C Black)
Merrily to Bethlehem (A&C Black)
Carol Praise (Marshall Pickering)
World Praise (Marshall Pickering)
Songs of Fellowship for Kids (Kingsway)
Every Colour under the Sun (Ward Lock)
Hymns Old and New (Kevin Mayhew)
David, Roger Jones (Christian Music Ministries)

Books

Colours of God, Diana Murrie (BRF, 2003)
Stories of Everyday Saints, Veronica Heley (BRF, 2002)
Sharing Life through Advent, Jenny Hyson (BRF, 2004)
Special People, Special Places, Janet Marshall (BRF, 2005)
Collective Worship Unwrapped, John Guest (BRF, 2005) (some more seasonal material)
Easy Ways to Seasonal Plays, Vicki Howie (BRF, 2000) (includes a play for Harvest for 3–7s)
Living in a Fragile World, Peter Privett (BRF, 2003) (exploring conservation and citizenship for KS2)

Multi-Sensory Prayer, Sue Wallace (SU, 2000) (includes ideas for Creation, Christ the King and Advent)

The Lion Prayer Collection, ed. Mary Batchelor (Lion, 1996)

Dramatised Bible Readings for Festivals, ed. Michael Perry (Marshall Pickering)

In Time of War, ed. Anne Harvey (Blackie, 1987)

A World War II Anthology, selected by Wendy Body (Pelican Big Book and small format) (Longman, 1998)

Saying Goodbye to Greg, Christine Chapman (BRF, 2004)

Grandma's Party, Meg Harper (BRF, 2003)

Wonderful Earth, Nick Butterworth and Mike Inkpen (John Hunt, 1990)

A Short History of Nearly Everything, Bill Bryson (Black Swan, 2004)

Oriel's Diary, Robert Harrison (SU, 2002)

A Busy Time for Angels, Martin Cox (John Hunt, 2001)

The Works: every kind of poem you will ever need for the literacy hour, ed. Paul Cookson (Macmillan, 2000)

The Works 2: poems on every subject and for every occasion, Brian Moses and Pie Corbett (Macmillan, 2002)

Contact details

Christian Aid
PO Box 100
London SE1 7RT
020 7620 4444
www.christian-aid.org

The Royal National Lifeboat Institution
West Quay Road
Poole BH15 1HZ
0845 122 6999
www.rnli.org.uk

Send a Cow
The Old Estate Yard
Newton St Loe
Bath BA2 9BR
01225 874222
www.sendacow.org.uk

Christian Music Ministries
325 Bromford Road
Hodge Hill
Birmingham B36 8ET
0121 783 3291
www.cmm.org.uk

The Imperial War Museum
Lambeth Road
London SE1 6HZ
020 7416 5320
www.iwm.org.uk

The British Legion
48 Pall Mall
London SW1Y 5JY
020 7973 7200
www.britishlegion.org.uk

Websites

www.coventrycathedral.org.uk
www.dti.gov.uk/fireworks
www.google.com (search 'images' for many useful pictures)
http://puzzlemaker.school.discovery.com/code/BuildWordSearch.asp
www.ashmolean.org/ash/objectofmonth/2002-11/theobject.htm
www.charitychoice.co.uk
www.nationalgallery.org.uk (click on 'Collections' and then enter
keywords in 'Search')
www.standards.dfes.gov.uk
www.qca.org.uk